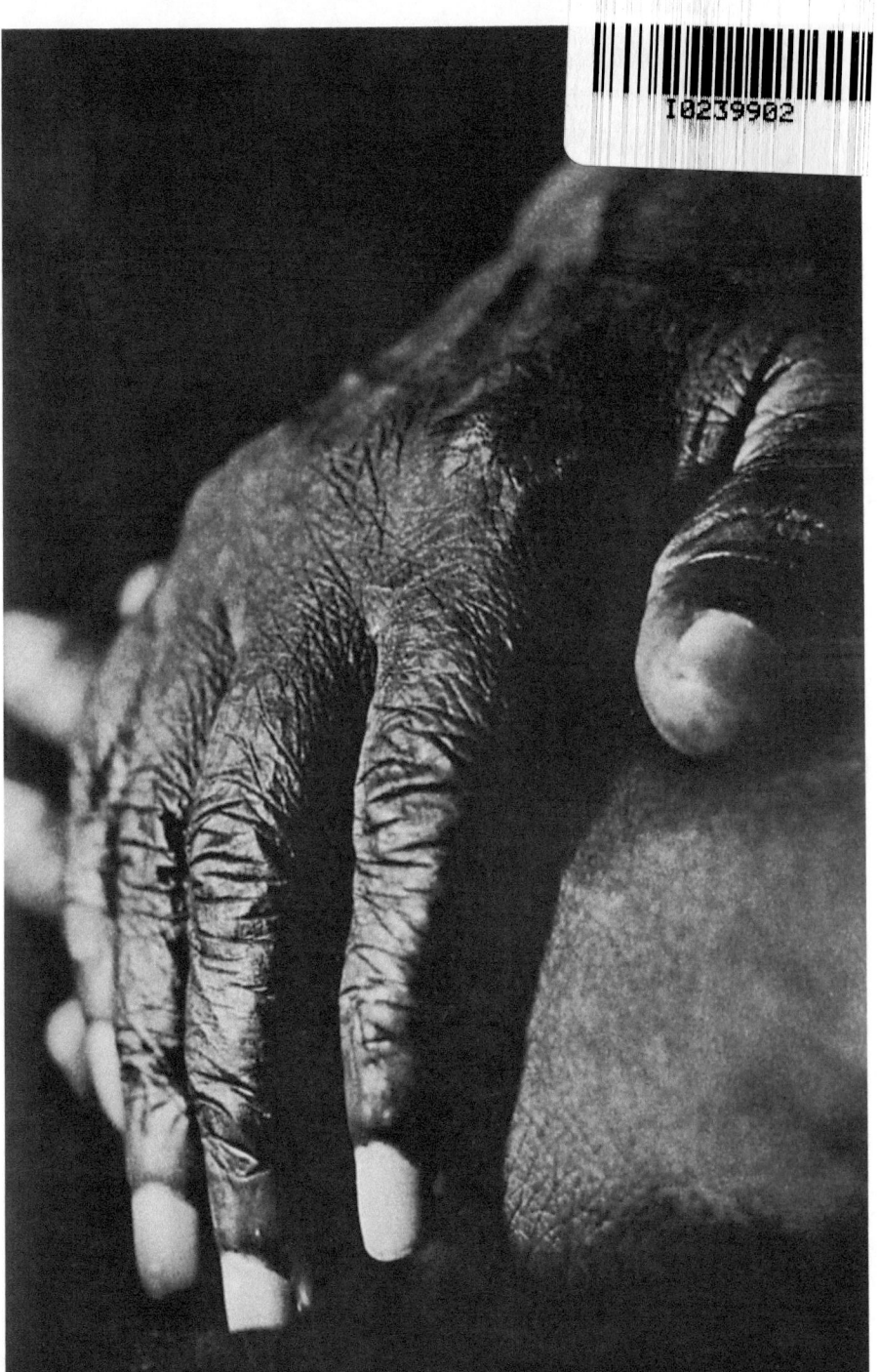

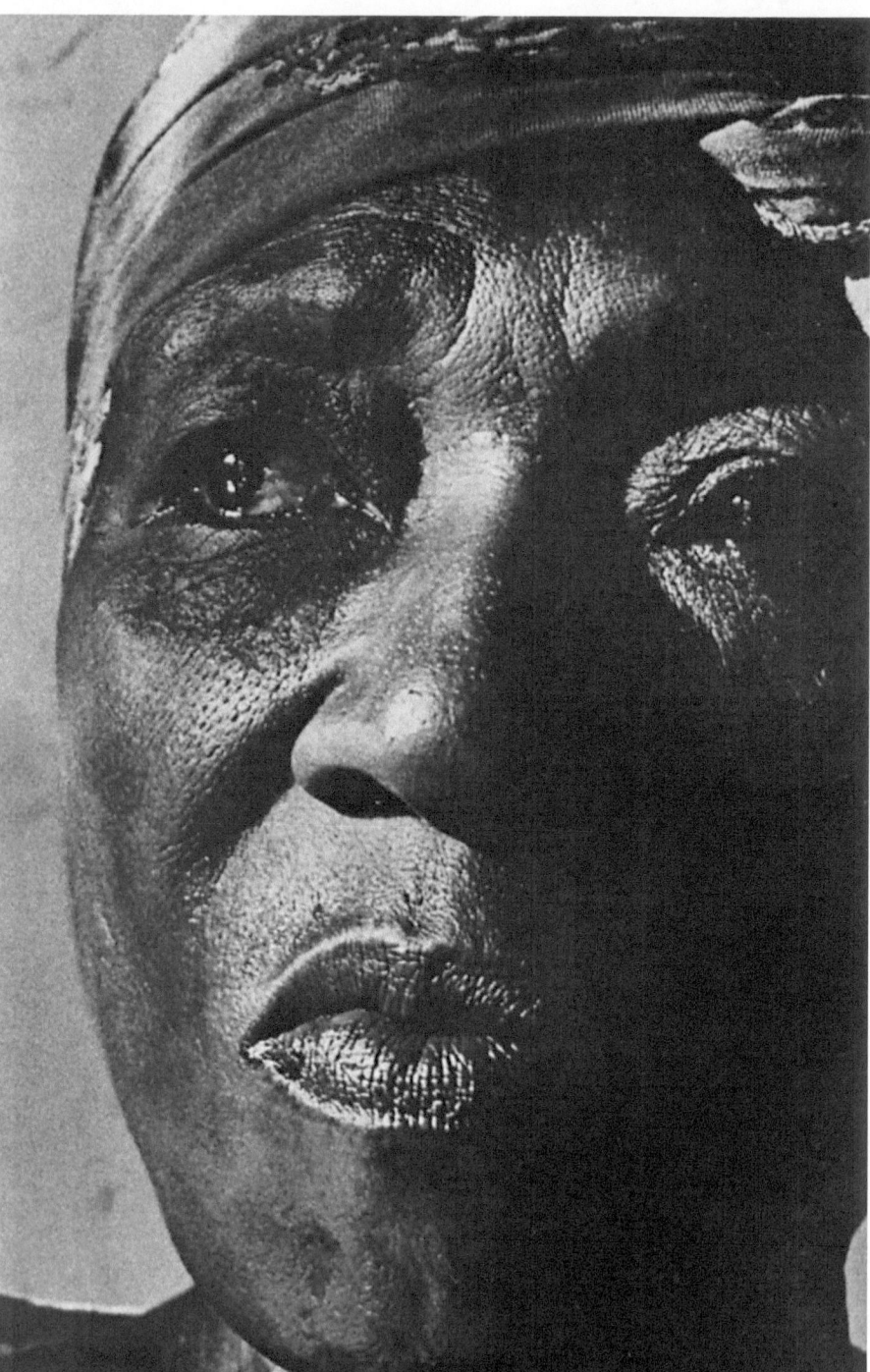

MISSISSIPPI NOTEBOOK

CIVIL RIGHTS IN MISSISSIPPI
Trent Brown, General Editor

MISSISSIPPI NOTEBOOK

NICHOLAS VON HOFFMAN

PHOTOGRAPHS BY HENRY HERR GILL

INTRODUCTION TO THE NEW EDITION BY
CHARLES W. MCKINNEY JR.

UNIVERSITY PRESS OF MISSISSIPPI / JACKSON

The University Press of Mississippi is the scholarly publishing agency of
the Mississippi Institutions of Higher Learning: Alcorn State University,
Delta State University, Jackson State University, Mississippi State University,
Mississippi University for Women, Mississippi Valley State University,
University of Mississippi, and University of Southern Mississippi.

www.upress.state.ms.us

The University Press of Mississippi is a member
of the Association of University Presses.

Any discriminatory or derogatory language or hate speech regarding race,
ethnicity, religion, sex, gender, class, national origin, age, or disability
that has been retained or appears in elided form is in no way an endorsement
of the use of such language outside a scholarly context.

Copyright © 1964 by Nicholas von Hoffman
Originally published by David White Company, 1964
Reprinted by University Press of Mississippi, 2025,
by agreement with the Estate of Nicholas von Hoffman
Introduction copyright © 2025 by Charles W. McKinney Jr.
All rights reserved
Manufactured in the United States of America
∞

Publisher: University Press of Mississippi, Jackson, USA
Authorised GPSR Safety Representative: Easy Access System Europe -
Mustamäe tee 50, 10621 Tallinn, Estonia, *gpsr.requests@easproject.com*

Library of Congress Cataloging-in-Publication Data

Names: von Hoffman, Nicholas author | Gill, Henry Herr, 1930–2025,
    photographer | McKinney, Charles Wesley, 1967– writer of introduction to
    the new edition
Title: Mississippi notebook / Nicholas von Hoffman ; photographs by Henry
    Herr Gill ; introduction to the new edition by Charles W. McKinney Jr.
Other titles: Civil rights in Mississippi
Description: New edition. | Jackson : University Press of Mississippi,
    [2025] | Series: Civil rights in Mississippi series | Originally
    published by David White Company, 1964 | Includes bibliographical
    references.
Identifiers: LCCN 2025032282 (print) | LCCN 2025032283 (ebook) | ISBN
    9781496860835 hardback | ISBN 9781496860842 trade paperback | ISBN
    9781496860859 epub | ISBN 9781496860866 epub | ISBN 9781496860873 pdf |
    ISBN 9781496860880 pdf
Subjects: LCSH: Civil rights—Mississippi | African Americans—Civil
    rights—Mississippi | African Americans—Segregation—Mississippi |
    Civil rights workers—Mississippi | Civil rights
    movements—Mississippi—History—20th century | Mississippi—Race
    relations—History—20th century
Classification: LCC E185.93.M6 V66 2025 (print) | LCC E185.93.M6 (ebook)
LC record available at https://lccn.loc.gov/2025032282
LC ebook record available at https://lccn.loc.gov/2025032283
British Library Cataloging-in-Publication Data available

CONTENTS

Series Editor's Note VII
Introduction to the New Edition IX
Foreword 3
June and July 17
August and September. 51
Afterword. 122

SERIES EDITOR'S NOTE

THE CIVIL RIGHTS IN MISSISSIPPI SERIES presents important historical texts with a commitment to both scholarly rigor and respect for all readers. Each volume reproduces the original sources faithfully while being edited to align with the University Press of Mississippi's house style and current usage. Racial slurs have been elided, and terms such as *Black* have been capitalized in accordance with contemporary standards. At the same time, a commitment to historical fidelity means such language cannot be omitted entirely; readers encounter the past as it was written, with only these limited changes made.

INTRODUCTION TO
THE NEW EDITION

CHARLES W. McKINNEY JR.

IN THE SUMMER OF 1964, civil rights activists who'd been working in Mississippi brought several hundred mostly white college students to the state in one of the most compelling civil rights actions of the decade: Freedom Summer. The event was a moment of culmination for movement activists who'd been working in the Magnolia State since 1961. In the early years of the decade, activists working in the state had been unable to gain any national traction for a movement whose tentative successes elicited waves of violence perpetrated against organizers and the home-grown allies who assisted them. In the face of unremitting violence, activists on the ground decided (after considerable debate) to turn to America's most precious commodity for help and heightened publicity: white, middle-class college-age students from elite institutions around the nation. In the summer months of 1964, nearly one thousand students responded to the call to serve and converged on Mississippi to conduct freedom schools, open community centers, and register Black Mississippians to vote.[1]

For white Mississippians, Freedom Summer—an endeavor that, quite literally, flooded the state with "outside agitators"—amounted to a declaration of war. Across the state, white folks prepared for what many conceived of as a version of Armageddon. In the weeks before volunteers arrived, the state doubled the number of state troopers. The state legislature passed curfew laws specifically designed to curtail movement activity. Active membership in the Klan rose dramatically. Of the state's eighty-two counties, sixty-four of them burned crosses on a single night.² After a three-week period of training and orientation, students made their way to Mississippi, where they were met by private citizens, public officials, and the leaders of institutions far and wide—all of whom worked to maintain a racial status quo forged over the course of the past two centuries.³

The idea of Freedom Summer is the stuff of legend. If you didn't know what a "freedom summer" was when you first read about it in a book or on a computer screen, the sheer audacity and scale of the scheme would lead you to think it was the plot of an expensive Hollywood movie, a rendering of some mythopoetic drama. For ten weeks in the summer of 1964, this elemental confrontation played out across Mississippi, carried to the nation by a small army of reporters. The actors in this drama lived up to their billing. The determination, vision, and audacity of freedom summer participants was almost always matched by the reactionary, repressive efforts of state-sanctioned officials and private citizens who attempted to disrupt their efforts with bureaucratic hurdles, massive resistance, and violence. It should come as no surprise that Freedom Summer was one of the most reported-on events of the year.

Editors at the *Chicago Daily News* sent thirty-five-year-old Nicholas von Hoffman down to Mississippi to cover the summer project. From June through September, von Hoffman wrote a series of articles from across the state, chronicling the perils and prospects of the people engaged in Freedom Summer. *Mississippi Notebook* is a compilation of those articles, written during what Hoffman calls, mildly, a "distracted summer."⁴ Although von Hoffman had been hired by the *Daily News* as a labor reporter, his vocational odyssey to that point prepared him to report from the epicenter of the nation's civil rights struggle. As a resident of the South Side of Chicago in the early 1950s, von Hoffman helped create a mutual aid association for recent immigrants who were frequent targets of harassment and economic exploitation. Von Hoffman's rough-and-tumble organizing efforts caught the eye of Saul Alinsky, the famed community organizer and director of the Industrial Areas Foundation. Alinsky hired von Hoffman as a community organizer and put him to work for the Woodlawn Organization. Von Hoffman spent nine years as IAF's associate director and became one of Alinsky's closest allies.⁵

In the years before the *Brown v. Board of Education* decision, von Hoffman's work in a meatpacking plant "whetted an interest in learning about the people who lived on the other side of the wall that separated the black and white races in Chicago." This interest led him to begin visiting Holiness churches on the South Side in order to acquire a better understanding of Black working-class life. Partnering with sociologists from the University of Chicago, von Hoffman's intellectual foray into understanding Black life took him down South, where he conducted research on Black Holiness churches in rural Mississippi, Alabama, and Tennessee.[6] By the time he arrived in Mississippi in the summer of 1964, von Hoffman had spent years working with exploited immigrants, African Americans who lived in "wretched" housing, and a coterie of "ordinary people picking a way through the physical ruins toward a better life." These experiences certainly shaped his views on state power, race, and the transformative potential for collective action.[7]

When von Hoffman began reporting from Mississippi in June of 1964, he did so from the epicenter of the freedom struggle in the nation. As Bob Moses, one of the architects of Freedom Summer, famously remarked, Mississippi represented "the middle of the iceberg."[8] However, while the middle of the iceberg remained hard, cold, and virtually impenetrable, activists worked mightily in preceding years to bring heat, light, and change to the state. The decade began with the sit-in movement in February of 1960. This student-led movement spurred the mass mobilization of Black college students throughout the South. The Freedom Rides in 1961 further nationalized Black folks' quest for equality, modeling the type of constitutional confrontation that would, over time, compel the hand of the federal government. The Birmingham campaign in 1963, coupled with the March on Washington, further facilitated the massive increase in public pressure and nonviolent direct action across the South and the nation. As always, these bold assertions of Black humanity and self-determination were countered with state-sanctioned repression, delay, and violence.[9]

The movement's trajectory across the first years of the decade shapes the context for von Hoffman's *Mississippi Notebook*. In his clear, crisp prose, von Hoffman introduces Freedom Summer as the central battlefield in the movement at that point. He does not use the term "battlefield" lightly. For von Hoffman and the other reporters trying to make sense of what they saw, the language of war is not only appropriate—it is necessary to clearly stake out the level and depth of opposition at play. To this end, *Mississippi Notebook* begins by broadly sketching out the terms of engagement in the state. Von Hoffman brings the reader into the story by introducing us to the tentative white Mississippians who agreed to talk with him upon his arrival in the state. These snippets of dialogue and commentary provide us an initial sense of the complexity of the struggle in which we are about to be immersed. Even after a century, white Mississippians were little prepared for the changes being forced upon them by shifting national and international politics and the movement growing in the state, nurtured by a muscular outside assistance. Von Hoffman's interview with a white doctor from Hattiesburg gives us a sense of the conflict roiling within some folks in the state: "I know we've had a hundred years. I know that, and I'm ashamed to ask it, but we need more time. If we had more time, we'd work it out. I'm sure we would. I still have faith in the people of my state." For many whites in the state, this "faith," as *Mississippi Notebook* makes clear, rested on a curious mix: the accommodation of massive resistance and the hope of change at a glacial pace.[10]

Throughout *Mississippi Notebook*, the moderate impulses articulated by a smattering of the state's citizens, while present, were almost always dwarfed by a louder contingent of citizens: those determined to maintain the racial operating system that ruled the state since before its inclusion in the nation. From the day after the *Brown v. Board* decision in 1954, the state of Mississippi did not use its time to create better conditions for its Black residents. Rather, it used that time, in von Hoffman's words, to "equip and perfect every organ of government and virtually every private institution to fight any favorable change in the position of the more than forty percent of the population that is Negro."[11] For many white residents, the implication that the state would *eventually* have to enforce the Constitution amounted to a "treasonable" offense.[12] Von Hoffman doesn't sugarcoat this assessment. It is stark and unflinching, and it is a necessary and effective way to frame his reporting. *Mississippi Notebook* is a compelling entryway into Mississippi circa 1964.

Von Hoffman's organizing experience made him well prepared to plumb the complexities of movement building in Mississippi. His exploration of all of the moving parts of the freedom struggle provides a layer of depth to the storytelling that pulls the reader in. Early in the book, he introduces the reader to the debates and dialogues shaping the actions of the civil rights organizations working across the state. But, even with the benefit of this previous experience, reporting on the varied, frequently shifting terrain of the movement was not without difficulty. Newspaper editors expected their reporters to tease out the organizational distinctions between the national civil rights organizations, almost all of which were operating in the state under the banner of the Council of Federated Organizations (COFO).[13] Also, national organizations worked with homegrown groups that may or may not have had any official affiliation with national groups. Similarly, reporters needed to understand and relay the differing and frequently shifting relationships between white organizations such as the Citizens' Councils, the Mississippi Sovereignty Commission, and an assortment of other official, formal, and informal white groups. Local law enforcement agencies, sheriffs, and police chiefs added another layer of complication and confusion to the mix. Lastly, the federal presence in the state—FBI agents and representatives of the Justice Department—added more contingency and uncertainty to the protean events on the ground and how best to relay those events to readers across the nation.[14]

Just as von Hoffman rendered a nuanced view of the political terrain of white society, he also gave his readers a glimpse of the titanic choices confronted by summer volunteers and their homegrown allies as they expanded the movement in the state. *Mississippi Notebook* gives the reader a local-level view of the trial-and-error activists engaged in as they confronted the state's racial apartheid. SNCC's entrance in 1961 had been a small but significant move into the state. While their initial voter registration campaign in McComb saw small but meaningful gains, the mass arrest of high-school students and the murder of Herbert Lee forced SNCC to cease its fledgling efforts before they could establish a foothold in the state.[15] The arrival of Freedom Riders in 1961 in Jackson served as another beacon of possibility for the movement. Efforts to register Black folks to vote were tentative at best, frequently meeting with violence, but the work continued. In 1963, the movement's halting gains took a blow in the wake of Medgar Evers's assassination. The NAACP, the state's leading civil rights organization, reeled from the loss of its most effective leader. However, the work continued in dynamic and innovative ways. In November 1963, COFO organized a statewide "Freedom Vote" in an attempt to mobilize Black voter participation and to show the nation that Black folks were, in fact, deeply invested in one of their central constitutional rights. Over eighty thousand Black Mississippians cast a ballot. The momentum generated by the Freedom Vote laid the groundwork for Freedom Summer.[16]

Von Hoffman brings a healthy skepticism when it comes to the transformative power of bureaucratic organizations; you can see that hesitance peek through in the early pages of *Notebook*. Unions, civil rights organizations, churches—they all carried both potential and problems in the push for social change. But this hesitance—such as it is—doesn't inhibit von Hoffman's ability to explicate and explore a foundational aspect of the movement at this point: Freedom Summer activists were attempting to confront an investment in racial subordination that operated on a molecular level in the state. Moses's reference to the state as the "middle of the iceberg" was not hyperbolic. Who do you call when the people shooting into your house in the dead of night are deputy sheriffs? Voting is arguably the most fundamental tool to effectuate structural changes in your society, but who do you contact when, after trying to vote, you along with several of your relatives, get fired from your jobs after the local paper reports on your efforts? Where do you go, how do you respond, and what does it look like to create a viable movement designed to confront what von Hoffman called "every oppressive custom" in the state?[17] And what happens when the people tasked with enforcing the status quo are officers of the state, or are in charge of the state's central institutions? In order to *begin* contending with the scope and necessity of Freedom Summer, von Hoffman brings us back to this crucial starting point. At one point in *Notebook*, von Hoffman asks whether the scope of Freedom Summer is "radical?" Does the action, and the rhetoric deployed to articulate its aims and goals, constitute something we could call radical? Yes, von Hoffman tells us. As he relays in *Mississippi Notebook*, the audacious scope of Freedom Summer and the incendiary words utilized in its support are the inevitable responses to the state's determination to keep its Black citizens mired in poverty, poor health, and ignorance.

Von Hoffman's framing also explicates the ambitious scope of Freedom Summer: COFO hoped to build a summer-long initiative that would address these fundamental barriers to Black life and build upon what organizers in the state called the "slow and respectful work" of building a sustainable movement. The initial hope of bringing a thousand young people from across the country actually wound up being something closer to six hundred. Yes, it was an invasion force. And yes, that force was organized only after activists who'd worked across the state in the first years of the decade faced the hard realization that the beating, imprisonment, and murder of Black Mississippians did not (and perhaps would never) engender any sort of statewide or national response to the issues those martyred individuals hoped to change. In unambiguous, precise prose, *Mississippi Notebook* relays the titanic task that stood before the civil rights consortium and those who sought to confront and change the state.

As events in Mississippi unfolded over the summer of 1964, coverage of the moment tended to focus almost exclusively on the confrontations between summer volunteers and recalcitrant white Mississippians. This was to be expected; the conflagration brewing in the state produced a nearly endless supply of stories about bravery, terror, state action, and activist responses. While *Mississippi Notebook* gives readers a ground-level glimpse of the local people and activists who worked together during the summer, von Hoffman also made an intentional effort to chronicle the *totality* of the initiative. From the mundane to the murderous, von Hoffman took pains to relay the full range of experiences he encountered.

Mississippi Notebook provides a window into the ebb and flow of movement work, giving readers a glimpse of hopeful, vibrant humanity shadowed by fear and violence. He writes movingly of Freedom Summer volunteers and local townspeople across the state. In Natchez, Freedom Summer volunteers sing to a group of Black children a few feet away from a building blown into rubble by local terrorists (who got the address for the civil rights headquarters incorrect and inadvertently blew up the wrong building). After handing out a thousand leaflets and knocking on dozens of doors to advertise an upcoming evening civil rights meeting, volunteers hoped that five people would attend, as that would constitute a "win" for the moment. However, the sheriff and his crew stop everyone from entering the church except for movement workers. We see instances like this one play out repeatedly across the state in the book. Each time, we are witness to the mix of bravery, apprehension, and fear felt by volunteers and local supporters.[18]

Von Hoffman reports with clarity about the siege mentality that gripped Mississippi officials and citizens, while also providing his readers a view of the complicated responses of the many white Mississippians who simultaneously resisted efforts at integration but shunned the violence that laced the state's response. Reporting from the state also carried a risk. Von Hoffman doesn't shy away from the apprehension he and his fellow reporters felt as they are followed by police officers one evening for a full hour after an aborted meeting. In this instance, as in others throughout the book, the police presence is overwhelming and always potentially violent. Police departments across the state were riddled with Klan members, so the thin veneer of civil society frequently gave way to harassment or worse. In an instance that we see repeated throughout the book, duly elected sheriffs of a town were all too quick and happy to overpolice and harass Black folks but were hard-pressed to solve the "mysterious" bombings of civil rights offices, the homes of Black movement supporters, or the homes and offices owned by white residents who failed to exhibit sufficient fervor for segregation. Von Hoffman also conveys the sense of tentative optimism felt by volunteers. How did this small group of volunteers and their local hosts in Natchez respond to this first, failed attempt? By planning a second meeting, this time earlier in the day, while also ensuring that the police didn't find out about it beforehand. Von Hoffman writes movingly about Chico, a Freedom Summer volunteer, weeping as he describes the event: "It was beautiful. Thirteen people came. . . . They said they'd come to the next one. Thirteen people. It was beautiful." Slow and respectful work indeed.[19]

Von Hoffman's front-line reporting is a powerful corrective to oversimplified national narratives about the movement to that point. One powerful example of this is the way he chronicles the tenuous relationship many rural Black Mississippians had with the tactic and philosophy of nonviolence. Nonviolent direct action and passive resistance constituted core elements of the training that volunteers received before making their way to Mississippi. This should come as no surprise: after all, the "N" in SNCC did stand for "nonviolent." Nonviolence represented, for many, a bedrock principle of the civil rights revolution. By 1964, the images of peaceful Black protesters, dressed in Sunday finery as they withstood withering attacks from cops, dogs, firefighters, and enraged private citizens had been seen around the world. The sit-ins, Freedom Rides, Birmingham, and a host of other flashpoints reinforced the usage—and the power—of the tactic.[20] For COFO organizers in Mississippi, this represented an essential part of the process of social change. Since the beginning of the student-led phase of the movement in 1960, the tactic of nonviolence took on an outsized role in the construction of civil rights narratives. With so much of the early scholarly work on the movement focusing on Martin Luther King and his steadfast commitment to nonviolence, it was almost inevitable that nonviolence became viewed as the only tactic deployed by movement folks.

Mississippi Notebook reminds its readers that the introduction of nonviolent direct action into rural Mississippi was a complicated task—one that frequently did not end in success. The principles of nonviolence ran head-first into the realities of deeply entrenched violence. Writing on the casual nature of white violence perpetrated against Black folk, Charles Payne remarked in his classic study *I've Got the Light of Freedom* that frequently the point of the violence was that "there did not have to *be* a point." People were killed for political activity, for being too slow on the road, for owning land, or for no reason at all.[21] However, in the face of rising violence and an imperative for nonviolent direct action, von Hoffman noticed and chronicled the ways local people throughout the state engaged the nonviolent paradigm on their own terms. Working with Freedom Summer volunteers, local folks countered Klan meetings and cross burnings with church meetings and continued movement efforts.

They also responded to the threat of violence by arming themselves and keeping guard over their family and their property.

Von Hoffman shows and reminds us what the admixture of nonviolence and self-defense looked like on the ground in the summer of 1964. In his reporting, he took great care to show how violence—real or potential—shaped the day-to-day choices and decisions of freedom summer workers, local activists, and folks in any way affiliated or associated with the movement. Given the context of this violence, and the way violent outbursts would rarely be investigated or discouraged by local law enforcement, von Hoffman shows us how the choices of local people and their allies *make sense*. Throughout *Mississippi Notebook*, von Hoffman introduces us to people who made the best choices they could in the wake of violent acts or in anticipation of them, choices that had little regard for ideological purity. In the weeks before the court-ordered enforcement of school integration in one small town, whites in the city burned a cross and shot into several homes owned by Black folks. Local Black farmers responded by arming themselves. Von Hoffman also observed how activists in the city began posting armed guards in front of the local community center they'd erected to conduct freedom meetings. One farmer, who possessed a considerable amount of land, "sits by night hidden in the back of his farmhouse with pistol and rifle when things are tense." His reporting on these facts is intentionally unremarkable. Von Hoffman doesn't sensationalize these potential confrontations. In his prose, these responses are conveyed in a matter-of-fact manner: farmers milk their cows, carpenters sharpen their tools, and activists defend themselves from terrorist attacks. These are not decisions forged in rage. Rather, as von Hoffman shows us, they are the choices many (if not most) rational people made in the face of unremitting violence, particularly at a time when local law enforcement had no intention of protecting folks who spoke out.[22]

Freedom Summer folks made choices that reflected a simple fact: nonviolence as a response to racial terror was *always* a tenuous proposition. As historians of the movement would observe in books written in subsequent years, rural areas in the state were frequently the most vulnerable when it came to establishing and maintaining a nonviolent ideological position. In these spaces, von Hoffman noted, the "idea of nonviolent resistance is passing fastest." This uncertainty and doubt was not only reflected in the opinions of home-grown activists; civil rights workers trained and steeped in the philosophy also expressed their uncertainty, and in many places stopped advocating it altogether. "You could see the guns on the front seats of cars as people drove to night civil rights meetings," Hoffman writes. In addition to arming themselves, Black folks also, on occasion, took care to inform the local authorities that if "someone" approached their property with ill intent, that they were armed and prepared to defend themselves, their families, and their property. After being warned about a potential attack, one freedom fighter sought out the county sheriff and told him plainly: "I'm gonna defend my home." In this and other exchanges, *Mississippi Notebook* shows the reader that, even as people verbally challenged the idea of nonviolence, their actions revealed less of a *rejection* than a *recalibration*: Mississippi activists remained nonviolent with the people who engaged with *them* nonviolently. Von Hoffman's book, this first draft of history, powerfully chronicles the rich, variegated responses to nonviolence in Mississippi in the 1960s. It will take historians and other scholars of the movement several decades before the literature of the movement reflected the varied ways local people contended with and remixed the concept of nonviolence on the ground.[23]

In an effort to fully render Mississippi's turbulent terrain, von Hoffman met with a host of white folks who'd been born and raised in the Magnolia State. To that end, *Mississippi Notebook* explores the varied responses of white people to the movement, revealing a landscape that, while thoroughly shaped by segregation and white supremacy, reflected the tensions and fissures extant in the state at the time. At no point does Hoffman shy away from the first facts of white life in the state: the steadfast political adherence to segregation that, though varied, shaped every aspect of the state. As von Hoffman shows throughout *Notebook*, one version of political moderation in Mississippi is a white person who believes that, while segregation *may* be a problem, it would be best to give the state another *century or so* for it to make its way beyond the institution. To illustrate another strain of moderation, von Hoffman introduces us to an anonymous Mississippian who tells him: "We need outside help. We need the Civil Rights Act. We need law and sense, and we need it more than we need segregation, and I'm a segregationist." *Mississippi Notebook* lays bare these contradictions throughout. Of course, this is no form of "moderation" at all; scores of white folks across the state were driven out of business, or driven out of the state, for expressing the merest inclination to enforce federal civil rights legislation.[24]

A critical mass of the reporting coming out of Mississippi in the summer of 1964 focused on the violence perpetrated against activists across the state. This is certainly the case in the wake of the disappearance of three civil rights workers—Goodman, Schwerner, and Chaney—early in the summer.[25] The stories and images flowing from the state and into the nation's newspapers and evening newscasts constructed a grim and compelling narrative of the brutality faced by both out of town rabble-rousers and homegrown activists. *Mississippi Notebook* stands out for its insistence on situating the violence squarely in the realm of institutional authority. When members of the Jackson Chamber of Commerce suggested that its members "obey the new civil rights law" recently passed by Congress and signed by the president of the United States, a state senator replied on the floor of the Mississippi House: "We in Mississippi will put you back in line when you get out of line." Von Hoffman uses this ominous salvo to shape/frame the ways in which even the *possibility* of adherence to the law would be met with staunch resistance. He then shows us the varied nature of that resistance—from the rhetorical to the mass-based to the violent.[26]

Von Hoffman's focus on state-sanctioned power illuminates the internal workings of the state's power structure, showing the reader just how tricky it can be to change the workings of a state. Von Hoffman's reporting rejects the oversimplified portrayal of the white opponents to racial equality, frequently painted as pot-bellied rednecks. To von Hoffman, a thoroughgoing exploration of the state's political composition revealed "a land being warred over by bands of competitive factions, each of which is forced to be more extreme so as not to be outdone by the next."[27] Citizens' Council members (middle-class business owners) were dedicated to the principal of white supremacy and engaged in economic warfare against their enemies—Black or white. The Klan—secretive, organized, and violent—also pursued efforts to maintain a racial status quo. The State Sovereignty Commission, Mississippi's white supremacist version of the FBI, employed surveillance, counterintelligence, and intimidation to disrupt efforts to enforce the Constitution. While each of these groups shared similar aims—the maintenance of white supremacy—their methods and tactics spanned a range. These schisms and divisions complicated the convoluted path to racial equality. White supremacy, as von Hoffman reminds the reader, was a many-headed hydra. The maintenance of white supremacy was never actually about a solitary group of "whites" allied against "the Blacks." Rather, the maintenance of white supremacy more resembled something akin to state-sanctioned asymmetrical warfare. Von Hoffman captures the protean nature of this dynamic throughout the book, always keeping an eye on the ways in which the state's systems and structures shaped the terrain of the battles being fought across the state.

In the years after Freedom Summer, von Hoffman would go on to have a productive, provocative career as a journalist, commentator, author, essayist, and television personality. He worked at *The Washington Post*, spent a few years on *60 Minutes* in the early 1970s, and wrote weekly columns for *The New York Observer* and *Architectural Digest*. While at the *Post*, his reporting on Watergate and the shenanigans of the Nixon administration earned him praise and scorn on a national level. He recorded hundreds of radio commentaries for *Byline*, a show hosted by the Cato Institute. His most famous book, *Citizen Cohn*, a best-selling biography of Roy Cohn, chief counsel to Senator Joseph McCarthy during the anticommunist crusades of the 1950s, was made into a movie in 1988. When he died in 2018, journalistic venues across the political spectrum paid tribute to him as a trenchant truth-teller, one who was unafraid to traverse political boundaries in pursuit of clear, honest words.[28]

While von Hoffman may be more well known for his subsequent work, his first book, *Mississippi Notebook*, remains a powerful entryway into the tumultuous summer of 1964. His on the ground reporting—and his willingness to contend with the internal conflicts, structural challenges, and *irresolution* of movement work—makes *Notebook* an indispensable volume. Almost immediately after its publication, it became a valuable reference for movement scholars, political writers, and anyone interested in the slow, deliberative process of social change emerging out of Mississippi and other Southern states in the middle of the last century. *Notebook* reveals to us the liberatory possibilities forged in Mississippi in the summer of 1964. As von Hoffman states powerfully toward the end of the book, "The Negroes still don't vote, yet it is a changed state."[29] As von Hoffman understood, far from being only a moment of culmination, Freedom Summer was, in many ways, the *beginning* of a new phase of the movement in the state and nation.

The republication of *Mississippi Notebook* is very well timed. During the hot, violent summer of 1964, while the nation grappled with questions of race, social change, and the meaning of democracy, Nicholas von Hoffman provided us a glimpse of the battle for freedom and the multiplicity of fronts upon which activists waged that battle. *Notebook* gave us a front-row seat to see the perils and prospects of changing a society from within, with the notable assistance from outside forces. It revealed the depth of Mississippi's (and the nation's) investment in an antediluvian racial code and the extraordinary measures required to *begin* confronting that code on every level of society. The book introduced us to local and out-of-town folks engaged in acts of outright heroism and forced us to contend with the fear coerced by state power. With any luck, the act of revisiting *Mississippi Notebook* will remind us, once again, that in order to build the society we seek, we will need to take stock of our democratic commitments and obligations and drag the nation—kicking and screaming if necessary—toward the greater freedom we still seek.

NOTES

1. There is a vast literature on Freedom Summer and the organizing apparatus responsible for its creation and implementation. Several foundational texts include Howard Zinn, *SNCC: The New Abolitionists* (New York: Haymarket Books, 2013); Clayborne Carson, *In Struggle: SNCC and the Black Awakening of the 1960s* (Cambridge: Harvard University Press, 1995); Charles Payne, *I've Got the Light of Freedom: The Organizing Tradition and the Mississippi Freedom Struggle* (Berkeley: University of California Press, 2007); John Dittmer, *Local People: The Struggle for Civil Rights in Mississippi* (Urbana: University of Illinois Press, 1994); Wesley Hogan, *Many Minds, One Heart: SNCC's Dream for America* (Chapel Hill: University of North Carolina Press, 2007); Laura Visser-Maessen, *Robert Parris Moses: A Life in Civil Rights and Leadership*

at the Grassroots (Chapel Hill: University of North Carolina Press, 2016); Bruce Watson, *Freedom Summer: The Savage Season That Made Mississippi Burn and Made America a Democracy* (New York: Penguin Group, 2010); Faith S. Holsaert, Martha Prescod, Norman Noonan, Judy Richardson, Betty Garman Robinson, Jean Smith Young, and Dorothy M. Zellner, eds., *Hands on the Freedom Plow: Personal Accounts by Women in SNCC* (Urbana: University of Illinois Press, 2010); Sally Belfrage, *Freedom Summer* (New York: Viking Press, 1965); and Nicole A. Burrowes and LaTasha Levy, "Freedom Is a Constant Struggle: Teaching the 1964 Mississippi Freedom Project," in Hasan Jeffries, ed., *Understanding and Teaching the Civil Rights Movement* (Madison: University of Wisconsin Press, 2019), 144–58. See also "Freedom Summer," directed by Stanley Nelson Jr., Firelight Media, January 2014. Important web resources include: SNCC Digital Gateway, accessed November 24, 2023, https://snccdigital.org/; and Civil Rights Movement Archive, accessed November 23, 2023, https://www.crmvet.org/.

2. SNCC Digital Gateway, accessed November 25, 2023, https://snccdigital.org/events/freedom-summer/.

3. On the training session received by volunteers, see Alice Lake, "Last Summer in Mississippi," in Clayborne Carson, ed, *Reporting Civil Rights, Part Two: American Journalism, 1963-1973* (Philadelphia: Library of America, 2003), 230–50.

4. Nicholas von Hoffman, *Mississippi Notebook* (New York: David White, 1964), acknowledgments.

5. Nicholas von Hoffman, *Radical: A Portrait of Saul Alinsky* (New York: Nation Books, 2010), chapter 3.

6. *Radical*, 46–48; Nicholas von Hoffman and Sally W. Cassidy, "Interviewing Negro Pentecostals." *American Journal of Sociology* 62, no. 2 (1956): 195–97, http://www.jstor.org/stable/2773352; Von Hoffman, *Mississippi Notebook*, 9–10.

7. Von Hoffman, *Radical*, 1–20.

8. Bob Moses, "Letter from Magnolia Jail," *The Liberator* 1, no. 2 (November 17, 1961): 3–4.

9. On the early sit-in movement and its impact, see William Chafe, *Civilities and Civil Rights: Greensboro, North Carolina, and the Black Struggle for Freedom* (New York: Oxford University Press, 1981); Brian Suttell, *Campus to Counter: Civil Rights Activism in Raleigh and Durham, North Carolina, 1960-1963* (Macon: Mercer University Press, 2023); and Julian Bond, *Julian Bond's Time to Teach: A History of the Southern Civil Rights Movement* (New York: Beacon Press, 2021). On the Freedom Rides, see Raymond Arsenault, *Freedom Riders: 1961 and the Struggle for Racial Justice* (New York: Oxford University Press, 2011). On the Birmingham Movement, see Glen Eskew, *But for Birmingham: The Local and National Movements in the Civil Rights Struggle* (Chapel Hill: University of North Carolina Press, 2000); Taylor Branch, *Parting the Waters: America in the King Years, 1954-63* (New York: Simon and Schuster, 2007); Diane McWhorter,

Carry Me Home: Birmingham, Alabama: The Climactic Battle of the Civil Rights Revolution (New York: Simon and Schuster, 2001); and Andrew Manis, *A Fire You Can't Put Out: The Civil Rights Life of Birmingham's Reverend Fred Shuttlesworth* (Tuscaloosa: University of Alabama Press, 1999). For a grass-roots perspective on the Birmingham movement, see "People in Motion": https://www.crmvet.org/info/bham_pim.pdf.

10. Nicholas von Hoffman, *Mississippi Notebook*, 3. On Black responses to white notions of the pace of change, see Charles W Mills, "White Time: The Chronic Injustice of Ideal Theory," *Du Bois Review: Social Science Research on Race* 11, no. 1 (2014): 27–42. https://doi.org/10.1017/S1742058X14000022; Julius Fleming Jr., *Black Patience: Performance, Civil Rights, and the Unfinished Project of Emancipation* (New York: NYU Press, 2022).

11. *Mississippi Notebook*, 4.

12. *Mississippi Notebook*, 4.

13. The Council of Confederated Organizations (COFO) was the umbrella entity created in 1961 to better coordinate movement action throughout the state. It included the Student Nonviolent Coordinating Committee (SNCC), he National Association for the Advancement of Colored People (NAACP), he Congress of Racial Equality (CORE) and the Southern Christian Leadership Conference (SCLC). On the impact of ideological diversity in the movement, see also *Mississippi Notebook*, 6–17.

14. On the multiple moving parts that constituted civil rights reporting, see Gene Roberts and Hank Klibanoff, *The Race Beat: The Press, The Civil Rights Struggle, and the Awakening of a Nation* (New York: Vintage Press, 2007), 364.

15. On the McComb movement, see the SNCC Digital Gateway, accessed November 28, 2023, https://snccdigital.org/events/bob-moses-goes-to-mccomb/; Payne, *I've Got the Light of Freedom*, chapter 4.

16. On the assassination of Medgar Evers, see Myrlie Evers, William Peters, William Morris, *For Us, The Living* (Jackson: University Press of Mississippi, 1996). On the Freedom Vote, see Robert P. Moses and Charles E. Cobb Jr., *Radical Equations: Civil Rights from Mississippi to the Algebra Project* (Boston: Beacon Press, 2001), 70–73, and the SNCC Digital Gateway, https://snccdigital.org/events/mississippi-freedom-vote/ (accessed December 3, 2023).

17. *Mississippi Notebook*, 6.

18. *Mississippi Notebook*, 58–63.

19. *Mississippi Notebook*, 57–63. The reference to "slow and respectful work" comes from Payne, *I've Got the Light of Freedom*, chapter 8.

20. A small sample of works on nonviolence as a tactic and philosophy include James M. Lawson Jr., *Revolutionary Nonviolence: Organizing for Freedom* (Berkeley: University of California Press, 2022); Anthony Siracusa, *Nonviolence Before King: The Politics of Being and the Black Freedom Struggle* (Chapel Hill: University of North

Carolina Press, 2021); Wesley Hogan, *Many Minds, One Heart: SNCC's Dream for a New America* (Chapel Hill: University of North Carolina Press, 2013); David Dennis Jr. and David Dennis Sr., *The Movement Made Us: A Father, a Son, and the Legacy of a Freedom Ride* (New York: Harper Paperbacks, 2023); Faith S. Holsaert, Martha Prescod, Norman Noonan, Judy Richardson, Betty Garman Robinson, Jean Smith Young, and Dorothy M. Zellner, eds., *Hands on the Freedom Plow: Personal Accounts by Women in SNCC* (Urbana: University of Illinois Press, 2010), part 5.; Laura Visser-Maessen, *Robert Parris Moses: A Life in Civil Rights and Leadership at the Grassroots* (Chapel Hill: University of North Carolina Press, 2016). For the vigorous debate about the limits of nonviolence, and the internal discussions related to the nonviolence/self-defense debate, see Akinyele Omowale Umoja, *We Will Shoot Back: Armed Resistance in the Mississippi Freedom Movement* (New York: NYU Press, 2013); Akinyele Umoja, "1964: The Beginning of the End of Nonviolence in the Mississippi Freedom Movement," *Radical History Review*, no. 85 (2003): 201–26; Charles E. Cobb Jr., *This Nonviolent Stuff'll Get You Killed: How Guns Made the Civil Rights Movement Possible* (New York: Basic Books, 2014); Christopher Strain, "The Ballot and The Bullet: Rethinking the Violent/Nonviolent Dichotomy," in Hasan Jeffries, ed., *Understanding and Teaching the Civil Rights Movement* (Madison: University of Wisconsin Press, 2019), 83–94; Charity Clay, "'Sincerely, Your Grandparents' Hands': Elucidating Similarities between the Trayvon Martin Generation of #BlackLivesMatter and the Emmett Till Generation of the Civil Rights Movement," in Francoise Hamlin and Charles McKinney Jr., eds., *From Rights to Lives: The Evolution of the Black Freedom Struggle* (Nashville: Vanderbilt University Press, 2024), chapter 1.

21. Payne, *Light*, 15.
22. *Mississippi Notebook*, 95.
23. *Mississippi Notebook*, 95. See note 20 above.
24. *Mississippi Notebook*, 44.
25. Dittmer, *Local People*, 246–48, 283; Watson, *Freedom Summer*, 87–100.
26. *Mississippi Notebook*, 43.
27. *Mississippi Notebook*, 45.
28. Robert McFadden, "Nicholas Von Hoffman, Provocative Journalist and Author, Dies at 88," *The New York Times*, February 1, 2018, accessed November 29, 2003, https://www.nytimes.com/2018/02/01/obituaries/nicholas-von-hoffman-provocative-journalist-and-author-dies-at-88.html.
29. *Mississippi Notebook*, 113.

MISSISSIPPI NOTEBOOK

FOREWORD

"I KNOW WE'VE HAD A HUNDRED YEARS. I know that, and I'm ashamed to ask it, but we need more time. If we had more time, we'd work it out I'm sure we would. I still have faith in the people of my state."

So speaks a Hattiesburg doctor, a Mississippian who describes himself to Northern visitors, but not his fellow townsmen, as a moderate. There are many like him in the state, men who know there must be change and are ready to accept it, and even work for it. When they ask for more time, they ask for it in the belief that the best hope for the best change for the state they love is through the actions of Mississippians themselves.

Yet in the spring of 1964 neither moderate nor anybody else in white Mississippi was able to bring himself to say that the century of grace had expired, that the time was up, and something would have to be done immediately. The most that people like the doctor could do was to extend themselves into a mournful and backward-looking sympathy for the hundreds of college students, ministers, doctors, and lawyers who were to come into the state to begin the revolution.

"I'm not questioning the motives of these civil rights workers," the doctor went on. "I've talked to some of them. I invited them to my office because I wanted to find out what kind of people they are. They made a good case for themselves.

"I talked to two of their ministers. I thought one was very sensible. I was impressed by what he had to say. The other was the 'but-but' type of person—always trying to break in with a 'yes, but.' I told him I thought he was too excitable, and he agreed maybe he was.

"You see, I know most of them coming into our state are fine people. I know they've come here to do what they think is right, but they don't know us. They're doing it the wrong way. They're forcing what can't be forced. We need time, though Heaven knows we haven't put the time we've had to much use."

In fact, a case could be built to show that Mississippi has put the time since the 1954 Supreme Court school desegregation decision to quite effective use. The time has been used to equip and perfect every organ of government and virtually every private institution to fight any favorable change in the position of the more than 40 percent of the population that is Negro. The time has been used to cauterize the society against the effects of change when, as at the University of Mississippi, a Negro was enrolled by the United States Army.

In the interval between 1954 and the spring of 1964 it became treasonable in this state—which thinks of itself as a sovereign nation in loose affiliation with the rest of America—to say that ultimately the Constitution will have to be obeyed. The years were spent displaying more Confederate flags and making speeches to gullible Mississippi white men about preserving the white race against foreign attack from Communist government officials in Washington and Communist bankers in New York.

Then, with the news that the civil rights movement would make its first great effort in the state this summer, the white population fell into a frenetic boil of emotion and activity.

A state legislator emptied a Jackson restaurant of customers by rushing in and shouting that a Negro cook had poisoned the food. Men armed and did close-order drill after work to protect themselves against the "rape squads" that they were sure would form part of an invading civil rights army.

Official appeals to let the authorities handle things "during this crisis" confirmed the people in their fears. It was to be a second Reconstruction, and the Mississippi folk memory of the first Reconstruction would have you think that every white family lost a plantation, and every white woman was ravished before the eyes of her menfolk, who were freshly and gallantly back from the war the South never really lost.

A white Mississippian wanting a calm description of the civil rights movement in the state or the projected Mississippi Summer Project would have found only two or three newspapers in the state to provide it. But the movement's true position and intention was so different from what white Mississippi imagined that few would have believed the truth even if they had been told it.

The winter of 1963–64 was a bad one for the young men and women who composed the full-time staff of SNCC (Student Nonviolent Coordinating Committee) in Mississippi. If they had not been beaten, they had been stopped. The stopping had begun the spring night in 1963 when a rifleman had murdered Medgar Evers as the state NAACP leader got out of his car. With his death the Jackson movement stopped.

SNCC had never been strong in Jackson, and it usually got along poorly with the NAACP. The town was always considered NAACP territory, but after Evers died, the NAACP was not able to get things moving again. The bullet had killed the strategically right man, and although there were riots after his funeral, they accomplished little save to make Medgar Evers better known in his grave than he had been before he was put into it.

They found Medgar's brother, Charlie, up in Chicago and brought him down to Jackson to take his place. Charlie, who acts as though he were glad to see you again even if he doesn't know you, made a bad impression on the people in the Mississippi freedom movement. They thought him vain and organizationally self-centered. They didn't trust him to live up to his part in agreements reached through the medium of COFO (Council of Federated Organizations).

COFO acts as the united organizational expression of all civil rights groups in the state. This includes not only SNCC and the NAACP, but also CORE (Congress of Racial Equality) and Martin Luther King's Southern Christian Leadership Conference (SCLC), plus a fluctuating number of purely local small-town and rural groups breathed into life by SNCC.

COFO had its beginnings in 1961 after the Freedom Riders had come into Jackson and McComb, gotten beaten up, and were jailed. That was when SNCC had also first come into the state, and when everybody was learning that Mississippi was able to stand impervious against coast-to-coast TV programs showing young people getting their heads bashed in trying to integrate a bus depot.

The recognition that the Negro people would have to be organized into a revolutionary force able to dispute every oppressive custom came as the tiny civil rights movement found that the more dramatic demonstrations won little beside thousands of dollars in bail and fines, and the enervation of months of litigation. As the new idea of what to do grew, so did COFO, a central unity based on broad and deep organization of all the Negro people and such few whites as might be willing to forsake family, friends, and position to live the life of a Mississippi "white n----r."

As federations of this sort go, the alliance has been cohesive, but it has not been able to abrogate the great differences in thought, membership, and method of the constituent groups. The differences have been the source of backbiting and organizational wrangling, which is looked upon by sympathetic outsiders and sometimes by the wranglers themselves as divisive weakness.

Yet the number of civil rights organizations, their great differences, and the impossibility of their agreeing on many fundamentals is a sign of the legitimacy of the revolution which they proclaim and carry out. This is not an artificial movement visible only to discerning intellectuals or a palace coup being contrived by a handful of political adventurers. It is a broad stirring of people, and as such is beyond the capacity of any single organized group to express or represent all of it.

A true revolution—that is, a true, abrupt change in the order of things inspired by the desires of many, many people—is not the work of one organization. The revolution of the place of labor in American life was led, particularly in the 1930s, by a number of organizations, some of whom hated each other with more energy, it would seem, than they hated their opponents, whom they styled "the bosses." Much the same can be said of the English, the French, and the Russian revolutions.

The COFO alliance has always been dominated by the radicals, that is, the young people. The NAACP has been fitfully present, thanks mostly to a Clarksdale druggist, Aaron Henry, the NAACP's state chairman, who is popular among the youth and has worked with them in a wholehearted way.

Unlike the NAACP, which really does have some membership in its branches here and there across the state, the SCLC has never been too important in Mississippi. Occasionally Dr. King or some of the ministers associated with him drop by, so to speak, and from time to time you may run across one of his staff workers, but the push behind the alliance has been the youngsters and their organizations.

The propulsive idea behind the alliance has been massive organization to carry out political, educational, and economic programs to give Negroes a material self-sufficiency to match and sustain the purely formal one of being able to vote or get a fair trial—assuming, of course, such rights are finally secured. Hence, the most driving rights groups have had only a casual interest in integrating restaurants when most of Mississippi's Negro people can't afford the price of the meal.

In Mississippi, as elsewhere, the NAACP subsists on the thin number of Negroes who have at least enough money to imagine making use of integrated motels, restaurants, and other places that people with coin in their pockets consider going. There are precious few such Negroes in Mississippi, so that when the youthful civil rights workers turned toward the untaught field hands and the pauperized menials who are the biggest majority, they necessarily began to think of large changes in the way society is run.

Their radical rhetoric and thinking has not been heard articulated by young lips in a generation or more in America.

That they should find support for their thoughts in the old radicalisms is not surprising. No group of people so closely resembles a proletarian class of the kind the nineteenth-century social thinkers described than Negroes in Mississippi. If they do not have the class consciousness of "workers," they have a consciousness of themselves as a people set apart.

They are a people set apart, and they have been taught to think of themselves as such. And, if business and businessmen anywhere in the United States are rapacious throwbacks to the businessmen that made radicals of thousands of Americans in the 1890s and the early 1900s, it would be this state's cheap labor business executives.

In fairness to the Mississippi businessman it should be said that no very great example has been set for him by Northern-controlled industry in the state or by Northerners who hold large blocks of stock in

Mississippi business. These Yankees have used neither their prestige nor their sometimes great economic power to press for change in Mississippi policy in government or private life. Since the Northern business interest often has no need to court local favor, but rather is the pursued party in the economic courtship, the failure to assume responsibility cannot be explained away as necessity or expediency.

The establishment of schools and social centers, and the attempts at medical and economic programs, which constitute the Mississippi Summer Project, arise from seeing the absurdity of gaining rights that almost no one can afford to enjoy.

The project's beginnings are also in the knowledge, won by costly test, that a segregated society like Mississippi's will not change with one blow or ten. Enormous power will have to be levered against it, and if much of that power, *faute de mieux*, will have to come from the North, it will only be called into Mississippi by a convincing demonstration that Negro Mississippians now demand a change. Moreover, should the power of the North be used to make Mississippi change, the change could not last unless Negroes were organized to take advantage of the change and retain their winnings. After the Civil War the Northern power was used, but inadequately organized and untrained Mississippi Negroes could not hold their own against the whites once the North had turned the other way.

Between 1961 and the fall of 1963 a start had been made toward the organization of Negro Mississippians into effective and abiding local groupings capable of carrying on political protest and other supporting activities, particularly in education. However, the mass of Negroes were still untouched by the organizational network that the civil rights alliance was trying to create.

Not that there had been no changes among the rural Negro population in recent years. There seems to have been some unmeasured and perhaps undefinable change at work among Negroes in Mississippi.

I remember traveling through some of the rural parts of the state in the early 1950s before the Supreme Court decision of 1954.

Then, without a proper introduction, I found that as an unknown white man I had difficulty establishing a reasonable human relationship with the rural Negroes I might chance to meet. They would "yessuh" and "nossuh" me, feign not understanding my questions, and beg money. But it was seldom they would risk having a discussion in which thoughts were honestly and equally exchanged.

The white man was too dangerous, and the idea of entering into such a relationship with him too foreign for most Negroes. But returning to Mississippi in 1963, it was plain that there had been a change. While there were still many Negroes who acted in the old way, there were also many who did not.

I noticed that even some country people, whom I might stop on the road, would talk full and fair once they recognized the hard accentuation of my Northern speech.

How the new ideas and attitudes started working their way into the rock of rural Negro society is a matter for speculation. It may have been the influence of the civil rights groups, although this isn't likely, because the summer of 1964 really marks the first time they have begun to have a wide contact with the Negro population; it may have been radio and television, but what TV plays is often bent to depict the white Mississippi view of things.

The change coming over the Negro people of Mississippi is probably much less than all-embracing. As late as the summer of 1964, James Forman, SNCC's executive director, could give a speech in Greenwood attacking the Negro churches there for refusing to provide space for a mass meeting at which Martin Luther King was to be the principal speaker.

Their refusal may demonstrate nothing more than that the cold fear of the white man remains and lives side by side with the new hope for liberation. It is a mistake to think that every Negro, or even most Mississippi Negroes, are ready to declare themselves publicly supporters of the revolution. Revolutions are usually, I suspect, the work of a small percentage of the people for whom they are being fought.

Nonetheless, the organizational development of the movement had ripened by the fall of 1963 so that the civil rights alliance could make its first state-wide effort, the running of a Negro, Aaron Henry, for governor. Since scarcely 5 percent of the eligible Negro voters in the state were registered, the alliance staged a private election in which it conducted its own "freedom" registration and "freedom" vote.

(Apparently nobody really knows how many Negroes in the state are registered to vote. The United States Civil Rights Commission has some figures but these statistics are out of date. The state of Mississippi, if it has accurate figures, doesn't let them out. The governor is on the state Election Board, but when I asked his office for figures, his public relations man said, "How the Hell should we know how many n-----s we got registered?" My impression is that most localities have allowed a few prosperous Negroes to register in recent years, but the number is a small fraction of what it should be.)

Some thousands of Mississippi Negroes took part in the campaign, which proved itself a worthwhile agitational device and attracted some national attention toward the state. It also foreshadowed the coming summer, when a group of Yale boys came down to help as volunteers during the campaign. They seemed to have spent a good part of their visit being chased by angry white locals, but most went back to New Haven strong in the conviction that they and many more must return.

By January of 1964 COFO was ready to try registering Negroes in big numbers. The place they chose to begin was Hattiesburg, county seat of Forrest County in the piney southeastern section of the state. The Hattiesburg choice was tactically sound. It is the governor's hometown and a federal court had ordered the circuit clerk (registrar) to let some Negroes register.

It was decided to get the drive going by having what COFO calls a "Freedom Day," a day when a large number of Negroes are persuaded to come down to the county courthouse, an activity that had, till that time, customarily resulted in instant arrest or trouble of some other kind. There is at least one attested case of a Negro being shot dead on the steps of a county courthouse as he entered the building to register.

The hope was that the combination of the court order and a good deal of national attention would, for once, get a significant number of Negroes on the rolls.

There is a dismal routine for trying to get a few Negroes registered in Mississippi, and it was put into effect at Hattiesburg. It will vary according to time and circumstances but, when possible, the idea is to recruit a large number of Northern clergymen to take part, thereby stimulating the interest of both the Justice Department and the press.

The clergy, in this case about seventy of them, duly arrived, followed by FBI men who set up motion-picture second-story windows to gather evidence in case anything bad should happen. The TV and newspaper people arrived in their turn, and on the day in question several hundred Negroes, reassured by the outside presences, made their try at registering.

Hattiesburg had decided it was not going to become a national *cause célèbre*. Instead of clubbing the picketing ministers or arresting the Negroes, it let the ministers march (a few, but not enough to make headlines, were arrested), and it allowed a few Negroes every hour or so to fill out the registration tests. There are no right answers for people of the wrong color.

Days passed while the ministers marched in the rainy cold weather and the Negroes stood in line down the courthouse steps waiting to be admitted to take the test which most would never pass in order that the whole dreary process might be repeated. It was a stolid kind of heroism, the middle-aged ministers tramping in the damp contracting rheumatism, and the Negroes being confirmed in their lifelong conviction that the Mississippi white man is a formidable white man indeed.

Jim Forman came over from SNCC national headquarters in Atlanta, Georgia, and tried to bait the Hattiesburg authorities into getting out their billy clubs to break the discouraging stalemate. One day he stood by the courthouse door with a tired-looking middle-aged Negro woman who, he said, had a constitutional right to wait inside out of the fitful showers. Seven months later, Forman would be in front of the Leflore County courthouse protesting that another woman had been beaten by the Greenwood police.

To no avail. Hattiesburg had learned from Laurie Pritchett, Albany, Georgia's police chief, that you can fight nonviolence with nonviolence and so avoid headlines as you consume the movement's slight resources for a long siege. Instead of putting Forman in jail, Hattiesburg retaliated by finding a half-crazy old Negro woman with a costume jewelry tiara to stand on the courthouse steps and rail inane incoherencies at the marchers and the waiters.

In the discouragement of Hattiesburg, cold, damp, and motionless people talked about opera *buffo* incidents, such as when a civil rights staff worker tried to place an FBI man under citizen arrest because the

FBI man would not arrest a Hattiesburg policeman who had arrested another civil rights worker.

"What were they going to do," asked the agent in charge when he heard about it, "take our guy down to SNCC headquarters and book him?"

It was a mildly amusing moment in the eventless tedium. For the onlookers who neither waited nor marched there was nothing else to do but to pass around any humor that could be scratched up. When a Hattiesburg policeman with the improbable name of John Quincy Adams said wonderingly of his German shepherd, "My dog's so mean he'd bite another police officer," the remark was laughed at for two days.

Not that the civil rights workers could find the byplay amusing. One of their number, a recent white Yale Law School graduate of stolid speech, was beaten up in the Hattiesburg jail by another white prisoner. The police chief said it was an "unplanned beating," i.e., it was done without official connivance from the top, but hardly without the jailor's knowledge.

The young workers and ministers were bitter about the FBI and the Department of Justice. Here they were in Hattiesburg with a court order requiring Negroes to be registered, and Negroes were not being registered while neither agency of the federal government appeared to be doing more than taking notes. The reason lay with the White House and the attorney general of the United States, who even at this writing cannot be accused of acting in reckless haste to protect Negro voting rights in the state.

The Mississippi point-scoring system is a strange one. When the civil rights people said they had won a victory by forcing the authorities to allow the obnoxious picket line to remain in front of the courthouse, no one was disposed to dispute the claim. Nevertheless, after the effort of transporting the ministers from so far and paying the costs arising from all the minor arrests, it was plain most of the Negroes would not be registered.

The press, seeing that nothing ghastly was going to happen, of necessity withdrew. And while the attempt at Hattiesburg continued on a diminished scale, it had not opened the door to bigger organizational opportunities. A few weeks later, the failure of the winter was assured when the same thing was tried at Canton, with more arrests but the same results.

About the same time, SNCC in Atlanta committed an error for which the alliance in Mississippi was to suffer. They staged several desegregation demonstrations at which there was a good deal of nonviolent violence. Forman called it "creative confrontation," but the news people who saw it said it looked more like kicking, punching, and biting. (SNCC partisans protest this description as an exaggeration.)

Worse has probably happened on thousands of union picket lines, but the political position of the freedom movement is such that Negroes only win public sympathy when they are the beaten, not the beating, party. The consequence of Forman's "creative confrontation" seems to have been that SNCC's never terribly generous contributors stopped giving almost entirely.

By March the movement was enduring a Valley Forge in Mississippi. There were reports of SNCC kids living on peanut butter and scrounging for cigarette butts. Some began turning up at the homes of Northern sympathizers confessing that pure hunger had done what neither the Citizens Council nor the Ku Klux Klan had been able to accomplish— run them out of the state.

Meanwhile, planning for the Mississippi Summer Project went on. Buildings were found for social centers, schools, and headquarters groups. Living accommodations in the Negro communities were lined up for the expected summer volunteers. Along with this, a great volume of press releases and research reports were mimeographed on paper one suspects was paid for with IOUs.

Many of the eighty or so SNCC staff kids who previously had held positions of minor responsibility were trained as best they could to take hold in the organization which would be taxed as never before by the amount of work, the number of workers, and, of course, the white Mississippians. As summer drew near, both the scale of the project and some of the more elaborate ideas, like the touring repertory theater, were cut back or dropped. (Predictions of three thousand volunteers were made. In actuality about six hundred students and three hundred or four hundred other people probably took part. There were no readily available and accurate figures, thanks to the strain put on COFO's fragile communications system and the itinerant nature of some of the people who arrived on their own without notifying anyone.) But the program's essence—the teaching and the voter registration—was refined, and the volunteer students, teachers, lawyers, and doctors did sign up.

SNCC kids from Mississippi moved about from campus to campus telling in a matter-of-fact way of the problem, the job to be done, and the dangers. They were listened to, and from Harvard to Stanford some hundreds did raise the money they would need to spend the summer in dubious and strange conflict. At the same time, organizations like the National Council of Churches elected to ignore the "creative confrontation" aspect of things, and recognize that in Mississippi there was no one else for them to support except SNCC and COFO.

As it became known that there would be a summer project, the alarm was spread in the state that the "mixers" were preparing an invasion whose purpose was the destruction of Mississippi society. In truth, the "mixers" were prepared to destroy the state's society. Even Americans without sympathy for what Mississippians like to call "our Southern way of life" wondered if this was the right way to do it. Some doubted that Mississippi Negroes really cared to have the summer "invaders" cause an uproar for which they might have to suffer in the fall. These are unanswerable questions.

I met a girl in McComb who told me that it was the outside people who gave her the strength to resist Mississippi because now she knew she was not alone. I met Negroes who said they wished the kids had never come.

I doubt that most people are willing to suffer very much to be "free." The American colonists do not seem to have hated George III enough to suffer a war to be rid of him. Their leaders had other ideas though, and probably dragged them into which later times have judged to have been justified.

Whether the Negro people in Mississippi want to be free if they must suffer terrible fear, economic reprisals, and physical mayhem is problematic. Certainly some do, particularly the small independent Negro farmers in whom the spirit of revolution seems strongest. But I doubt if the poorest field hands in the Delta, whom the whites lovingly call "the blue gum n-----s," would choose freedom and strife over peace and subjugation. Yet even in the Delta some have, and more give signs of being about to.

Freedom has been chosen for them, however, perhaps by history, but assuredly by their leaders who, like most revolutionaries, tend to think that anyone who so much as brings up questions like these must be in the enemy camp.

Some people may find these observations on the civil rights leadership a substantiation of the charge that they are "agitators" who divide people and cause trouble. Those who head the civil rights movement in Mississippi and perhaps elsewhere are agitators and troublemakers.

Given the situation in Mississippi, might we not say that the proper and only function of leadership is division, agitation, and trouble? Wasn't this what St. Paul did in Greece and Asia Minor, and isn't this what all men who are convinced of the need of change do in societies which do not have the capacity to change themselves?

How are the young men of SNCC to be censured for training their followers to keep a closed mind, to refrain from allowing themselves to see their opponents' point of view when every public institution in Mississippi has done the same long before them? A better question might be why we all of us in America allowed the situation to degenerate to the point where no other politics but revolutionary politics verging on warfare is possible?

The young leaders are tough-minded men. They are not only capable of bringing the white students into the state as willing hostages, but they really did it. And who can damn them for it when it was, as they ceaselessly point out, the murder of two white workers at the summer's beginning that moved a nation which had not been moved by the murder of many Mississippi Negroes?

Thus, though I cannot blame them for the necessities under which they labor, I cannot be around SNCC leaders such as Forman, John Lewis, the national chairman, and Robert Moses, director of the Mississippi Summer Project, without remembering the old joke about the radical giving a street-corner speech:

"Comes the Revolution, comrades, and every night you will have shrimp cocktail, filet mignon, and strawberry shortcake."

"What if you don't like strawberry shortcake?" asks a voice in the crowd.

"Comes the Revolution and you *must* like strawberry shortcake," is the retort.

ACKNOWLEDGMENTS

Most of the material in this book, both text and pictures, first appeared in the *Chicago Daily News*, which has graciously permitted its reuse in book form.

Such errors, inaccuracies, and faults as the book may contain are the writer's responsibility. He can defend himself only by pleading that the work is, as its title says, a notebook, not a definitive history: however, the idea of describing the Mississippi summer of 1964 in this form and scope, a distinctly new direction for American journalism, belongs to the *Chicago Daily News*'s executive editor, Lawrence S. Fanning.

Would that every editor could give every writer the same understanding direction and comforting support.

I owe a like debt to our newspaper's city editor, Robert Rose, and his assistant, Dean Schoelkopf, both of whom worked long and, I suspect, trying hours discussing the manuscripts with me and preparing them for publication. Then too, I must thank my colleague, Lois Wille, for reading and criticizing the work and providing me with moral support when the whole thing looked impossible and inexorable deadlines were having to be met.

I should also like to thank Henry Gill, my Mississippi traveling companion, whose magnificent photographic portrait of the state appears in this book, and for his patience in putting up with my odd notions of where to go and whom to see.

Lastly, I should like to express my obligation to Karl Fleming of *Newsweek* magazine and Claude Sitton of the *New York Times* for so much valuable information and many hours of good companionship when it was sorely needed during this distracted summer.

Chicago, September, 1964

JUNE AND JULY

DEVIL'S DUST, the little wind-stirred geysers of dry earth that blow up between rows of cotton plants, puff here and there across the fields.

Two Negro women walk by the side of the highway. Their parasols protect them from the sun which even now in the early morning has laid down its heat over the Mississippi Delta.

The blues and reds of the women's cotton dresses are vivid. The orange umbrella atop the tractor moving down the rows of cotton plants is unfaded in the sun's summer light.

The Mississippi sun does not bleach. It brings out color and magnifies detail so that no man can mistake another.

The lean men of Mississippi are unmistakable. They pause at the gas pumps in front of roadside general stores, their lifeless eyes full of suspicion forcing your own to glance downward as you get out of your car.

In this summer the stranger is the enemy, and the men of Mississippi wait and watch for him. In khaki pants and straw hat they stand their watch against the civil rights workers across the Delta counties—Bolivar, Sunflower, Leflore, Tallahatchie.

By night they ride dipping roads in the hill country to where that fatal plant, the kudzu vine, grows everywhere strangling grass and tree. Along Route 19 they drive through Neshoba County's scrub oak and scraggly pine forests without headlights when the moon is bright and the mist is sparse and patchy.

At Natchez cars cross the Mississippi River bridge from Vidalia, Louisiana. The Negroes say they're loaded with guns. Confederate flags fly from their antennae, but no one really knows what they carry.

The little girl whose preacher father heads the Ku Klux Klan around Natchez answers the phone and says, "My daddy ain't here. He's off in town selling Bibles."

Up in Jackson, the state capital, the governor says, "A great resentment burns inside of me when I consider the distorted picture of my beloved state which is presented to America by her enemies."

For the Negroes, fear makes the night wakeful.

South of Tchula in Holmes County, a mocha-colored old Negro farmer finishes supper and checks to see if his rifle is where it belongs. Hartman Turnbow knows his Delta. There have been many nights since they firebombed his farmhouse that the courteous old man has stood watch.

Sixty miles away to the southeast, Negro farmers in the dirt-road community of Harmony check their guns and count their children as the night comes on. There are no phones in Harmony, and without them the short nights of summer are long, longer than ever now because the white civil rights workers are living hidden among the Negro farm folk.

Farther south, in Laurel, a tough Negro dentist with a reedy voice, Benjamin Murph, must see the straight-up Southern sun as it moves toward Louisiana and wonder if this is the night the Klan will make good the promise of death attached to the rock thrown through his window.

Every man watches and every man is watched.

The whites watch the Negroes. The Negroes watch the whites. The FBI, the State Sovereignty Commission, the newsmen, the Citizens Council, the Klan, the civil rights workers—all watch.

Before the summer and the coming of the hundreds of civil rights workers, they were watching each other because there is no trust left between the white man and the Black man. The "good Mississippi n----r" who played with the white folks' children and cooked the white folks' food and labored and loved the white folks and was loyal, if he ever existed, is gone.

Now there is a Black stranger in the white man's house.

But even while guarding himself against this new darkie who has treasonably and ungratefully turned against him, the white man cannot bring himself to believe it.

The white man is like the volunteer auxiliary policeman in Greenwood who had to take a day off from his business to stand guard while Leflore County Negroes tried, as they have so often before, to register to vote.

"Look at them fool n-----s," the man said as he fiddled with his uncomfortable steel helmet. "They can come on down here and register any day they want." Then looking at the line of a hundred or so Negroes standing in the sun, he went on, "There ain't one respectable Greenwood n----r on that line. They're doing it so's they get publicity.

"Why hell, look at that fat old n----r woman. She can't vote 'cause she can't read. There's white people in the county we don't let vote, lots of them.

"We got a lot of good colored people in Leflore County . . . n----r businessmen and n----r preachers. If our good n-----s want to vote, why ain't *they* standing up there hollering for their 'freedom'?"

A few feet away an old Negro man, his white straw hat contrasting with the richness of his very dark, almost black skin, answers a reporter's questions. A small blond boy stands next to his father listening.

The Negro says: "As long as they's only five or six come to register, it's all right, but when they's a hundred, they raise hell. . . . Anything that can kill a n----r or a dog—they put a gun on him. There's a law against everything 'round here, excepting it's open season on n-----s and snakes all year 'round."

The boy looks up at his father and asks, "Daddy, you hear what that n----r's saying? You hear what that n----r's saying?"

Does the father hear, or is he like the Mississippi father who is supposed to have taken his son to a Klan meeting "so the boy can learn about segregation while he's young"?

Some whites have come to recognize the rebellion welling up in the people they still refer to as "our n-gras." They are galled by it, though, like the vindictive Hattiesburg housewife who said, "When I saw that little colored girl of mine waiting in front of the courthouse with those common n-----s I couldn't hardly believe it. I would have let her go anyway. She was spending more time eavesdropping than cooking."

They used to say that Negroes knew more about white folks' business than white folks. It didn't matter if they overheard the family's secrets. They were "jus' n-----s."

Long before the Mississippi Summer Project brought Northern college kids tumbling into the state, the whites, whether they always admitted it or not, had come to know the Negroes had stopped being "jus' n-----s."

But knowing is not the same as accepting. A white plantation owner can still sit in a Greenwood bar and tell a visiting Yankee about "hoe cake," the corn and water patty that Negro field hands used to cook on the blades of their hoes for their noontime meal in the fields. The plantation owner talks as though hoe cakes, "chopping cotton," and pickaninnies having fish fries on the levee were still the life of the Delta.

Then came the kids. They had been recruited off the campuses of the greatest universities in the land—UCLA, Harvard, Stanford, Chicago, Cornell, Yale—but they knew nothing of Mississippi, her mood or her people. Before they had been in the state forty-eight hours one of them, and two full-time civil rights workers, were murdered.

The National Council of Churches had spent a small fortune setting up an orientation program for the students on the campus of Western College for Women at Oxford, Ohio. They brought the full-time civil rights workers up from Mississippi to train them and warn them about sheriffs' posses and the primitive plumbing.

Trained or not, the pious Congregationalist girls, the acidic anti-white Negroes from Northern slums, verbose sons of college professors, young romantics, adventurers, and idealists—all were hopelessly alien to Mississippi.

The people from Mississippi at Oxford tried to tell "what it is like," but they didn't know how.

George Green, who is twenty-one and has, as someone once said of him, "more bullet holes in his shroud than any other man in Mississippi," knows what it is like, but he hasn't words to convey it. For nearly a year he has been operating in the bad southwest counties where the Klan rides—Pike, Amite, Franklin, and Adams. He knows.

George is coffee-colored, thin and long and always pleasant answering questions. He has a bad stomach, but he says it was that way "before," meaning before his leaders began sending him to places like Natchez, where he got four bullets in the rear of his fleeing car one night.

George knows about Mississippi, but he can't tell about it so that it is believable to nice kids from Columbia.

Some are like Peggy Sharp, a round, brown girl from Indianapolis. She went swimming during training sessions at Oxford, and on the long drive south she giggled and told the other people in the car how frightened she was.

They assigned her to Holmes County where the hills break quickly off just west of Lexington and the Delta begins. They told her to find the Negroes living in the shacks with the corrugated iron roofs and persuade them to register.

She thrived. Her only complaint, when she would reappear from time to time in Jackson, all smiles, was about the shortage of bathtubs with hot running water up in Holmes County.

They came, as widely different each from the other as they were from Mississippi itself, and they broke the mood of the state.

Their reactions were Northern and defiantly unsubservient. Phil Moore, the Winnetka, Illinois, boy who graduated from Harvard this spring, reacted in anger to the beating he got.

Some may have wanted martyrdom, but not the young woman who was liberated after five days in a Greenwood jail. Her eastern woman's college manners betrayed her when she found out her hunger strike hadn't made the newspapers.

"They should have told us short hunger strikes aren't news. My God, I starved myself for five days!"

Ultimately more memorable perhaps is another young woman volunteer standing in the Vicksburg Freedom School showing the first paintings done by her small Negro students.

There are Freedom Schools, libraries, and community centers now in many parts of the state. For the first time a few of the children at least are in contact with well-educated people.

It is little enough, but amid the passion, the dramatic landscape of heavy foliage and pools of water, and ignorance, it is a hope for a new beginning.

The extra molecule in the Mississippi air—fear—attacks the central nervous system. It works on the optic nerve to distort what you see, on the auditory nerve to scramble what you hear, and on the cerebral cortex to paralyze and anger.

Fear attacks the nice white lady who works for the state House of Representatives. She hesitates to show a reporter a list of bills enacted by the legislature.

"Those civil rights workers have been coming up here trying to look up the law," she explains.

Fear is at work on Lynch Street, at civil rights headquarters in Jackson. The office is in a street-level store. The windows have been broken so often they are permanently covered with plywood.

A Volkswagen station wagon is parked in front.

Inside the wagon, kneeling and sweating in a great ganglion of wire and electronic equipment, is a young physicist on his vacation from Sperry Gyroscope in New York.

He is working on a radio communications net for the collegians canvassing the back country to get Negroes to dare to try to register to vote. The walkie-talkies and the two-way car radios are to be an early warning system against entrapment and attack.

"Two men ahead of me," says a voice from a walkie-talkie down the road from a civil rights radio car. "I think one of them has a club or a lead pipe or something in his hand . . . what should I do?"

"Run."

Fear turns some of the young people bitter and robs them of their better judgment.

A sign in the Jackson headquarters reads:

THERE'S A TOWN IN MISSISSIPPI CALLED LIBERTY.
  THERE'S A DEPARTMENT IN WASHINGTON CALLED JUSTICE.

Two white men stand under the awning of the J. C. Penney Company store in Philadelphia, watching a blue-gray Plymouth park by the Neshoba County courthouse.

"FBI," says the first.

"Federal Bureau of Integration, you mean," the second retorts.

Fear pushes the youthful leaders of the movement toward stubborn and heedless decisions.

They persist in accepting the free services of the National Lawyers Guild, although former Attorney General Herbert Brownell once called it a Communist front. And the rights movement's best friend, the National Council of Churches, has asked them to stay away from the Guild.

Jack Pratt, the Council's energetic lawyer, asked the civil rights leaders not to associate with the Guild, but they turned him down, and they love Pratt for his feud with Police Chief Ben Collins up in Clarksdale, and his tussles with a prosecuting attorney over in the southeastern part of the state whom even his friends call "acid head."

They have resisted similar pressure from the NAACP's Legal Defense Fund, too.

But they are not Reds. Their free-ranging social radicalism could never suffer the restrictions of Communist dogma. Yet a fear-born sense of isolation makes them politically obtuse and loyal to any friend who will stand and sing with them "Which Side Are You On?"

"Communism? What are you talking about, man?" asks a white college boy in the Meridian voter registration headquarters. Negro children come here to play ping-pong in a room set up for them by Mickey Schwemer, one of the three who were murdered in Philadelphia, forty miles away.

"Man, don't you know," the boy says, aping Negro idiom, "Communism was way back in the 1950s?"

Another boy, a socialist, remarks, "Sure, there are Stalinists here, but they're not running things."

A poised Reed College coed from Larkspur, California, speaks the words of lonesome courage, not collectivist inevitability: "I considered the possibility of being killed, but if we chicken out there'll be more violence. Social change must come from individual outcasts like us in Mississippi. We're more willing to take risks because we have less to lose here."

The experienced workers neither admire derring-do nor practice it. They play it safe, travel by day whenever possible, and follow a careful routine of telephone security checks.

They cultivate the art of escape: "Never go any places where there aren't at least two roads so that people who follow you in have to watch two exits when you leave."

Good fast cars and good fast drivers are much in demand. Heck (short for Hezekiah) Watkins, a slightly built, dark youth of eighteen, who says he started driving when he was five, is considered by his friends around Carthage and Canton to be the best driver in the Mississippi movement. They say that Heck can take the awful, unpaved back-country roads—even by night—at speeds up to one hundred miles per hour.

"I do it by touch of hand and eye," he will tell you. When it's all over and "freedom" is won, Heck, who got in the movement "when my mother encouraged me to do it because she wasn't able to," says he might try LeMans or Sebring.

One way to conquer fear seems to be by an overcompensating, taunting, plucky bravado.

I saw it in a good-looking Negro teenager who was about to go on a picket line in Greenwood and be arrested.

He clapped his hands and did a mocking bent-knee dance close to a policeman who was used to having his Negroes say "yessuh" with their hats in hand.

Another policeman saw the kid and said aloud to himself, "That's one n----r boy I want to get in the jailhouse."

Maybe the boy heard him, because he immediately began to sing a teasing song at the cop. A few minutes later he was on the picket line, and then he was one of a shrieking bus load of hysterical arrestees being taken to the jailhouse.

Some of the same audaciousness must live within the most experienced and calculating leaders.

James Farmer, executive director of CORE, lolled on a sofa in a second-floor sitting room of Meridian's Young's Hotel "for colored." The country was in an uproar over the murdered three (who were then only known to be missing), and up in Philadelphia the whites were out in their pickup trucks with their shotguns. It was no place for CORE'S executive director.

Farmer, who has a face like a chocolate moon and a stomach which oozes over his belt buckle, ate sandwiches, dipped into bags of potato chips, and told us, "I expect to go to Philadelphia and retrace the steps of the missing men."

The next afternoon he rolled up the road to the town, leading a six-car cavalcade of whites and Negroes, male and female. Far from getting his head blown off, the off-balance authorities protected him with highway patrolmen who cradled shotguns and submachine guns to use against their own people should they decide to attack.

That there can be safety in bold action is recognized by the theoreticians of nonviolence. One of them, the Reverend James Lawson, of Dr. Martin Luther King's group, explained this to some of the Northern college students before they came South this summer.

"When you turn the other cheek you must accept the fact that you will get clobbered on it."

But then he told them, "Harassment increases as nonviolence loses the initiative. In the midst of an attack you cannot be passive. Instead of using a fist or a gun, use your eyes, your voice, or some other means of confrontation [with your assailant]. I don't believe hiding your face is a good approach when being beaten because it tends to be more passive than actively nonviolent."

Probably no one, not even the people who have mastered themselves to suffer it, can explain quite how a man can nerve himself not to hide his face. The fear must be unspeakable.

The closest to a description I have heard came from a young Negro man, half-drunk, half-hip, half-crazy, who had bought a ticket on one Freedom Ride too many:

"Hey, get down there to Mississippi and get scared, then we can communicate. Hey, you people have got to understand it. Hey, this Mississippi isn't an easy state.

"Hey, I'm thinking about the man with a .45. Hey, I'm thinking about six slugs in your back. Hey, talk about dealing with the State of Mississippi, baby. They take you to jail, strip you, and lay you out on the floor and take a leather belt and beat you and beat you and beat you until you're almost dead.

"Hey, it's not too late to pull out. They shot out the windshield. They shot into the church. I know how white people think, baby. They ask you silly questions and they beat you up, baby.

"I went on a Freedom Ride from Nashville to Jackson once. I smoked three packs of cigarettes, baby, one right after another."

In Chicago they give you an award for registering people to vote.

IT IS A WEDNESDAY AFTERNOON, and McComb, like any Mississippi town on a Wednesday afternoon, is quiet.

No walkers on its hilly streets. The stores mostly closed. No one standing beneath their awnings.

The quiet is amplified by the slow heat waves rising from the vacant sidewalk in front of the city hall. The moisture in the hot afternoon air dampens all sound.

This is McComb, Pike County, rolling green country, Klan country, bad country. They warn you about McComb, and how quiet it is.

"McComb's the silentest town I know. They's so mean they don't even talk to each other." White men, segregationists, three counties away over in Lamar, tell you that.

The silence had been interrupted momentarily about four o'clock this same morning, but now it had reimposed itself. The noise had come from the bomb exploding against the side of the little white house where nine young civil rights workers and a minister were sleeping.

They had been sent down to McComb because of Allen Dulles, and because they are the kind of young people they are.

After three of their comrades had turned up missing, subsequently discovered murdered in Philadelphia, the president had sent Dulles, the old CIA guerrilla fighter, to the state to learn how bad things are and make a report. He went back to Washington and said the president should send more FBI men and that the young rights workers should stay out of the dangerous areas.

The president did and the young people didn't.

The rights workers had to go to McComb because it *was* one of the most dangerous places.

"To the extent we don't push, they are going to push us," said Portland Cox, a very dark-skinned young man from SNCC. Cox was stating a Mississippi truism: if the youngsters once show that there is an area too dangerous for them, an area they can be scared out of, they will be shot at and bombed until they have been chased all the way up to Memphis.

They had to go to McComb, danger or not, because SNCC has a score to even with this silent town where the Negroes can tell you terrible stories of midnight sadism.

For this is the section of the state where the "movement" started in 1961 when the CORE people were trying to integrate the bus depot and were being beaten by street mobs—that was before the Klan and the Association for the Preservation of the White Race (APWR) had come in and organized McComb into a tight silence.

That was when they ran sixteen-year-old Brenda Travis out of McComb. Brenda is a big Negro girl with gay eyes that show the memory of pain without hatred. She is nineteen now, but she still flirts with the boys as though she and they were scrimmaging football players.

She was one of the leaders of the high-school youths who tried to integrate McComb with sit-ins. They put her in a reformatory, and when they finally let her out, they told her to get out of town or they would put her in the penitentiary. This young political exile sneaks home to visit her family occasionally, but SNCC tries to keep her safe in Atlanta.

It was in the McComb vicinity that Bob Moses first tried to register Negroes to vote. Moses grew up in Harlem, but beat the rap and got a master's degree in philosophy from Harvard. In a social revolution led by huge-voiced men who thrill people with the King James Bible English they learned in a thousand Baptist churches, Moses is an outstandingly poor speaker.

He is perhaps the most trusted, the most loved, the most gifted organizationally of any Southern Negro leader, but his speaking voice sometimes breaks, his cadences are monotonous, and his words are unimaginative. He is only moving when he talks about Herbert Lee, which he does very often.

Herbert Lee, whom few remember, was a Negro farmer who worked in voter registration and was shot to death about twenty miles from McComb, also back in 1961. Moses has made Herbert Lee stand for every Negro who has ever been quietly slain in Mississippi, and Herbert Lee must have played a part in Moses's decision to go back.

When the young rights workers returned to McComb in July this year, the movement, for all that could be seen of it, had been extinguished in the silence.

In fact, though civil rights headquarters in Jackson said the youths were being sent in to conduct voter registration, their real instructions seemed to be to survive, just to live and prove they could not be scared out of coming.

After the bomb in the night, which woke up the mayor all the way across town, the silence had come back to McComb, and in the daylight it was more frightening because it was more unusual.

It made the noise of the dime dropping in the pay-phone slot seem so audible that I glanced across the street to see if anyone had heard and was looking at me. The busy signal coming out of the receiver was like a public alarm to get out of town.

The bombed house was still. The heat was awful, and noiselessness the more noticeable in contrast with the mumbled words passing between Jesse Harris and the FBI men who were interviewing him. Fatigue had made Jesse look gray instead of brown.

Two McComb policemen were in the front yard also. One of them looked at the hole and commented, "It looks like termites to me."

But their attention was fixed on a white Harvard psychiatrist who had come down from Jackson to offer what medical help he could. The police had warned him off the property, so he couldn't get in the house where the rights workers were. In fear and agitation, he walked up and down the dusty street, dabbing his sweating neck, and looking first at the police and then at the house.

"I don't know what to do. Should I go in?" he asked in words carried by hissing breath.

One of the cops said, but not loud enough for him to hear, "I'd like to give him psychotherapy in the basement."

Within the youths sat, stood, or lay down in demoralized fatigue. They seemed like the shattered planking of the damaged house. The town's silence had gotten to them, and they whispered or talked in low tones.

They said they were going to try to have a mass meeting of the Negroes that evening, but they were doubtful about many people being brave enough to come. Then, for a time we sat, three of us, in the living room with windows blown out and the curtains and the glass all over the floor.

"It's not the heat, it's the fear," a girl from Pittsburgh breathed.

I was afraid for them. I wanted to tell them to pull themselves together. Instead, I interviewed them, and they recounted how they had been asleep and dreaming thoughts of death just before they awoke to see the bloody face of one of the youths who had been wounded by the bomb.

Then small sounds could be heard in the back yard. Twenty youths, mostly Negro teenagers from McComb, were in the back sitting in a circle on the grass.

The leader, Jesse Harris, was there. In the depressing silence they were speaking low and slowly.

"What're we going to do?" one asks.

"It's a bad situation if we don't have the meeting," Jesse says, and they all fall silent.

"How are we going to get the people to come?" a girl wants to know.

"Give them the leaflets."

"Leaflets won't get them to come."

"Have to go talk to them."

"Visit your friends . . . parents, relatives," Jesse suggests.

"They'll say they'll come, but they won't be there. Ya know how it is."

"We just have to try."

Another very long pause in their talk, and then one asks:

"What're we going to do at the meeting? Shouldn't we have a song?"

Jesse asks them how many know the words to a freedom song. Most of them don't.

"We'll practice," he says.

A voice, low and unsure, tries to sing "Ain't Gonna Let Nobody Turn Me 'Round, Turn Me 'Round, Turn Me 'Round."

Most of the young people don't know the words. They pick up the melody raggedly and their beat is too slow.

They are poor singers, but the silence at McComb has been broken.

"JACKSON JOINS THE JET AGE," reads the caption above the picture of the new Allen C. Thompson Airport on the cover of the Mississippi capital's phone books.

Jackson normally attracts few visitors, so its jet-age airport has the spacious lifelessness of an underused railroad station. Jets are less common on its runways than coughing old DC-3s and 4s belonging to obscure airlines serving towns in Arkansas.

This summer, however, the airport has been the touchdown point for a wide and wild assortment of visitors—folk singers, congressmen, worried parents, and any number of people who escape easy classification.

Late in June, President Johnson's ambassador plenipotentiary to Governor Paul Johnson—Allen Dulles—arrived to become the first big-name visitor. The former head of the CIA is not well known in the state, so he didn't cause much excitement, but J. Edgar Hoover's arrival was another matter.

In a state where many of the citizens think impeachment is too good for the chief justice of the United States Supreme Court, and have serious doubts about the president's loyalty, Hoover is a rare personage, a popular federal official. In fact he is a kind of folk hero.

The mayor of Jackson and Colonel T. B. Birdsong, who heads the highway patrol, met Hoover at the airport. Everybody smiles. They took him to have a chat with the governor at his official mansion with the magnolia trees in the front yard, and they showed Hoover his fraternity's motto painted on the ceiling of the state Senate.

The venerable FBI chief looked at the Kappa Alpha words, "Dieu et les Dames" (God and the ladies), made an admiring noise, and said, "I didn't know about that, and I thought I knew all about the organization."

But when Hoover got down to the business he came for, opening a big new FBI office with fifty agents, the Southern hospitality thinned.

The governor was present for the occasion and he put the best possible face on it he could, but not even the many promises of reciprocal cooperation could change the facts.

Johnson, a thin man whose neck and face shoot out of his shirt collar so that he looks like a surprised ostrich, said he was "delighted" that all those new FBI agents were coming to Mississippi.

He didn't look delighted though, and seemed happier when he got to the familiar Mississippi boast that the state has the second lowest crime rate in the country.

If the figures didn't square with Hoover's presence in Jackson, the governor could explain that.

The state's industrial development program was beginning to pay off so that "Mississippi is no longer a cornbread and buttermilk economy. We will now begin to attract the top hoods and crooks of this country," he said, not without a trace of Chamber of Commerce pride.

The Yankee reporters, who also have to be counted among the summer visitors, decided that the additional FBI agents might hypo the state's economy, but not enough to lure the syndicate out of Chicago and Las Vegas.

"Mississippi industry," intoned a tired and possibly bitter newsman, "consists of a few runaway underwear factories from New Jersey and a possum lard-rendering plant."

The press and the FBI seem to have combined to make this a banner year for the Mississippi motel and car-rental business. This strange fraternity of Mississippi outcasts, disliked by both segregationists and integrationists, can be seen everywhere.

During their infrequent off hours, they complain half humorously about being away from home, about their bosses, the hostile rednecks and the arrogant young civil rights collegians.

A magazine cameraman grouses:

"Know what my picture editor told me? He said the Klan didn't scare him, an' that I should get a shot of them burning a cross in front of a Negro's house. Says he'd like the Negro on his knees begging and the Klan should have their pillowcases on . . . and in color yet."

An FBI man remarks, "If I don't get home and see my wife pretty soon, it's gonna be bad, very bad."

In Jackson's finest restaurant, two happy reporters tell the waitress to bring them a baked Alaska (usually served topped by a flaming sparkler) with a burning cross. She contrives to do so and the scandalized customers listen while the newspapermen loudly rename the dessert a "baked Alabama."

The visitors who get the most sympathy are the TV cameramen. There is no place they do not go, toiling after their announcers, carrying their cameras, which might as well be large red bull's eyes for the local stone-throwers. I remember one TV soldier, gone gray in the integration wars, drinking beer and cursing everything in sight.

"Don't tell me about these SOBs. See this?" he asks as he pulls up a trouser leg to show an almost healed scar.

"St. Augustine," he says, "and this one on my arm is Birmingham. You can't see the six stitches in my scalp I got at Ole Miss. All I'm hoping now is they don't send me to Harlem."

Other visitors: the young people from SNCC and CORE did not want the integrated party of NAACP national board members to test the public accommodations section of the Civil Rights Act. They were afraid the testing would cause violence against the college kids working in the Freedom Schools and on voter registration.

The NAACP group came anyway, the white Congregationalist lady looking morally unconquerable, the aggressive Negro labor leader wearing an old-fashioned, flat straw boater, a number of others, and Kivie Kaplan.

Kivie Kaplan used to be in the tannery business in Boston, but is now an aging, good-humored man whose heart belongs to the NAACP.

He arrived with his pockets full of little calling cards on which were printed the words: KEEP SMILING . . . KIVIE KAPLAN.

The reporters at the airport accepted his cards with astonishment. A room clerk in the Jackson Hotel that Kivie and his associates integrated accepted a card in silence. A deputy sheriff in Canton with a hard look on his face handed his back to the smiling old gentleman, who had stopped smiling.

The NAACP visit was a mild fiasco. The young rights workers often were barely polite to their touring elders. The hostility of the white natives grew with every mile of their trip, and, in Philadelphia, they just escaped being gunned down on the steps of the Neshoba County courthouse by several hundred farmers with revolvers you could see in their overall pockets.

In Meridian they fell to fighting among each other. Some of the group wanted to issue a statement attacking Mississippi and all her works, but the chairman, an aging head of a Los Angeles savings and loan association, wanted to get out of the state alive and then issue the statement.

Some of the parents of Northern college kids came to visit also. One was the father of a Yale boy, whose well-connected family had arranged through the good offices of United States Senator was James O. Eastland to have the young man provided with an around-the-clock state-police guard.

The boy was furious. He told his father it disgraced him in the young people's eyes. The father apologized and then went off to see one of the state's leading segregationists who had been a classmate of his at Yale. The man, he said, had assured him that things were not as bad as they had been painted.

The National Council of Churches officials quietly helped to guide him out of the state.

The most respected visitor was J. Robert Lunney, a New York lawyer representing an organization with the impossible name of the Lawyers' Committee for Civil Rights Under Law. The Committee is staffed by lawyers from some of the nation's most famous law firms. Lunney is a trim former naval officer and assistant United States district attorney. His services were donated to the Committee by his old-line firm which, like the others associated with the endeavor, had become concerned over the difficulties civil rights workers have in getting adequate representation in Mississippi courts. Lunney was able to move around the state charming nasty sheriffs and suspicious judges while he got ministers out of jail.

Largely through his diplomacy, the Mississippi Bar Association issued a statement saying it would see that all people, regardless of their politics, would be able to get a lawyer. Nobody thought the statement would cause many Mississippi lawyers to accept civil rights cases but in this place of primitive types the word is often confused with the fact, so that the mere statement was thought dangerous enough to be given very little publicity. It is always possible, as Lunney would remark, that if they said it, they might one day do it.

One of the most famous summer visitors was Dr. Martin Luther King. The mixed reception he got in the Delta town of Greenwood mirrors Mississippi divisions.

The police sent to the airport to guard him looked as though they would have preferred to shoot him. The one thousand Negroes in the hall where he spoke went wild cheering him as he entered—all, that is, except the young Negro SNCC workers.

They too were on their feet shouting, but if you stood close to them you could hear that they were not cheering him. They were shouting the derisive nickname they call him by behind his back. "De lawd, de lawd!" they screamed.

"WE IN MISSISSIPPI will put you back in line when you get out of line."

These words were spoken not long ago in the Mississippi Senate. They were aimed at the Jackson Chamber of Commerce because of its suggestion that its members obey the new civil rights law. But they apply to any white Mississippian who shows signs of sympathizing with what the legislature calls "creeping, amalgamating socialism."

Many Mississippians do show such signs.

The number is unknown, but a lot of white Mississippians are deeply troubled. They are also frightened, not by the Negroes or the civil rights movement, but by their fellow whites.

"If you print my name next to what I'm going to tell you," a member of the legislature cautioned me, "I'll be ruined. I mean flat-out ruined. I'm not talking about not being re-elected. I mean I'll lose my business, my friends. I'll be run out of this state, and it's the only home I know."

The politician, whom I had gotten to know over a long period of time, then said, "Don't let these guys [the other politicians] fool you when they say we can solve this situation if the outside agitators go home.

"I don't like the agitators any more than you'd like a bunch of unwashed, unshaved, banjo-toting kids with beards stirring up the colored people in your community, but they're right about one thing: We need outside help. We need the Civil Rights Act. We need law and sense, and we need it more than we need segregation, and I'm a segregationist."

He is not alone in what he thinks.

An upper middle-class woman sat in her living room, highball in hand, bracelets jingling as she gesticulated while speaking:

"I didn't want to admit it to myself. Neither did Harry [her husband], but the time came when we had to admit it: Our home isn't our own.

"There are people I'm afraid to invite into my own house because I recognize what would happen to us if people knew we had a known civil rights sympathizer here. I'm not a sympathizer, but the way we're going, we'll have martial law in our community."

I interviewed a businessman as he drove his car because, he said, "I'm fairly certain they don't have the car bugged." Then he told this story about himself:

"I'll admit to you I've made financial contributions to the White Citizens Council. It's not that I don't know better. I went to school at Northwestern.

"I resisted as long as I could the only way I could, by keeping my mouth shut and not supporting them. But there's only so long you can do that. Then some of the boys from the Council come around and want to know where you stand.

"I had to go along with them. I salve my conscience by having a friend up North send along my contribution to the NAACP—which I don't agree with either because of their extremism, but I hope it balances out."

The civil rights leaders like to talk about the Mississippi "power structure," a business-political alliance that is supposed to be able to run things pretty much the way they want in the state.

If, the civil rights argument goes, the "power structure" would pass the word, the fear would end and the progress would begin.

On first look at Mississippi the description is plausible enough. It does seem to be a land where all the Southern stereotypes come to life and form a monolithic society. The sheriffs, some of them anyway, do chew tobacco and talk about "runnin' that bad n----r out."

Former Governor Ross Barnett does talk like a night-club comedian's parody of a Mississippi governor. The newspapers do howl about "outside agitators," and everybody seems to have xenophobic paranoia.

But when you get closer to it, the state looks more like a land being warred over by bands of competitive factions, each of which is forced to be more extreme so as not to be outdone by the next.

The Citizens Council, the Klan, the APWR, and the State Sovereignty Commission seem to be as interested in destroying one another as the civil rights movement.

Beyond keeping segregation and suppressing dissent, they agree on nothing. No "power structure" controls them. In fact, the big businessmen and the civic-leader types seem to be powerlessly on the defensive.

You can see why when you get a look at a Klansman close up. The Klan in Mississippi is not the decadent, publicity-seeking organization it is in some parts of the South. In Mississippi it is truly secret and truly dangerous.

More out of curiosity than out of any real hope that he would tell us anything, I knocked Sam, the head of the Mississippi Klan, out of bed one morning about 9:30 or 10:00. There was no danger in it because Sam, who never dreamed any newspaperman knew of his existence, was too taken by surprise to do anything naughty.

He lives behind his slot-machine store, and when we got him out of bed his eyes were red-lined from the liquor of the night before. He whined his denials that he had any connection with the Klan in the incongruous speech patterns of a small child saying he didn't do it. But Sam had done it. Standing in his store, his cheeks nicked from the quick shave he'd given himself on our arrival and the night's liquor still about him, you could see that the respectable citizens, the members of the "power structure," would have a fine lot of influence over him.

He was frightened by us now, but we knew when we left he would try to find out how we got his name and take his revenge if he could.

The Mississippi Klan has a full-time man whose job is counterintelligence to make sure that just such leaks are calked.

The "loyal opposition" is an unheard of idea in Mississippi. Dissent is deemed subversion, so that no political faction, no public organization, exists between the civil rights leper colony and the orthodoxy of white supremacy.

Thus a system of political, social, and economic repression, designed to keep Negroes in their "place," has led to keeping whites in their place, too. That is why men like Dr. Martin Luther King speak of freeing the white people as well as the Negroes.

As in any totalitarian society, you do not buck the party line, and in Mississippi there is a party line which adults and children alike are supposed to memorize and believe in.

Here is a sample of it which comes from what the Citizens Council is asking to be made reading matter for third- and fourth-grade children:

God wanted the white people to live alone. And He wanted colored people to live alone. The white men built America for you. White men built America so they could make the rules. George Washington was a brave and honest white man. . . . The white man has always been kind to the Negro. . . . Negro people like to live by themselves. Negroes use their own bathrooms. They do not use white people's bathrooms. . . . This is called our Southern Way of Life.*

As a result of the national attention put on the state because of the Mississippi Summer Project, the Civil Rights Act, and a federal court order to integrate first grades in three parts of the state, some whites are laboring to turn Mississippi around and point it in the direction of the twentieth century.

Police protection of civil rights workers is better than it has ever been before. That may seem like sarcasm after three murders, more than a dozen church burnings (by the summer's end the score was closer to thirty), and no one knows how many beatings, but it is literally true.

Nonetheless, people who know the state best are skeptical.

A white, native-born doctor who may secretly be an integrationist describes recent Mississippi history this way: "Our political leaders, our business leaders, our press, and our churches have failed us. They have let the power and the influence go over to gangs of crazy people. Now they want to get it back, but they're afraid."

Mississippi towns make the familiar boast that they are communities of churchgoers, and they really seem to be. On Sunday mornings the churches are full of people.

In this rural state the churches, and perhaps the Masonic lodges, are often the whole of social life. Potentially no institution has more influence and uses it less than the church in Mississippi.

---

* This illuminating fragment was discovered and brought to light by James W. Silver. His book, *Mississippi: The Closed Society*, should be read by anyone who wants to have a full and serious understanding of the state.

Over the last ten years many Mississippi ministers have tried to influence the state to put a brake on the violence and the bitter-end opposition, but they have failed, and most of them have been forced out of the state.

A few heroic clergymen are left, like the Catholic priest whose house sits opposite a store owned by a Citizens Council leader. Four or five times a day this storekeeper comes out on the sidewalk with a bullwhip, which he cracks against the pavement as he stares across the street into the priest's living-room windows.

In many places the church has been taken over by white supremacists. The pastor of one Jackson church is a former photographer from the Citizens Council. And there are many stories of pastors who are rumored to be deputy sheriffs on the side.

Mississippi exemplifies the perils of trusting the preservation of personal liberty to individual valor rather than institutional strength. The state's recent history is a catalogue of brave men, especially Protestant ministers, who have walked the plank of individual martyrdom. They might still have been in Mississippi, had they been able to work together through the institutional strength of their church.

The Episcopalian Church, which did in fact see the social condition of Mississippi as more than a problem for the individual conscience, as one for the church as an institution, has been able to hold its own more successfully than most. Their united clergy has kept many churches open to Negroes when those of other denominations have been split and terrorized and captured.

Thus a Methodist church in Jackson suffered the humiliation of having one of its members arrested for trespassing on his church property of a Sunday morning when he was accompanied there by a Negro. The Methodist Church of Mississippi has produced any number of courageous ministers and lay people, but as an institution it has never seen the society as its institutional concern.

Then, too, there are churchmen who have been wholly absorbed by the society and mistake pietism for prophecy.

In Philadelphia, during the first days after the three civil rights workers had been killed, the minister of the town's largest church delivered a sermon attacking the outside press for besmirching his community's reputation. He had not a word for the rowdies running on his community's streets.

More often, though, clergymen wash their hands of the matter and say it has nothing to do with their ministry.

One minister from a community in southwestern Mississippi, which has had terrible racial trouble and where both the whites and the Negroes are armed and ready to kill each other, could only say, serenely: "My calling is not preaching a social gospel, but is first and foremost a sacred gospel. I look beyond the chaos which is around us today."

THERE WILL BE NO "After-Labor-Day Doldrums" on the Gulf Coast. This disquieting news comes from the Mississippi Gulf Coast Vacation Club in the form of a press release meant to attract "visitors who wisely wait until early fall (to) avoid the summer crush."

This year the Mississippi summer crush has been mostly posed of impecunious young civil rights workers, Justice Department lawyers, FBI men, and newsmen giving the state a lot of publicity, but not much of it has helped Mississippi tourism.

It's questionable that even the "new and exciting Six-Gun Junction addition to the Deer Ranch midway between Biloxi and Gulfport . . . with its badman-and-marshal shoot-outs" can best some of the live-ammunition "shoot-outs" the local hosts have been entertaining their summer visitors with.

A few weeks ago they had one in nearby Moss Point that was so realistically done, a young Negro girl ended her evening out in the hospital with a rifle bullet in her side.

World travelers who may have wearied of the Cote d'Azur should find a Mississippi vacation different.

If you decide to take the family car with Northern license plates, you may be stopped by the sheriff's police before you've gotten very far into the state.

The officer will politely ask you to state your business in Mississippi. Tell him you are a tourist. (It helps to be able to produce a wife and a few small children to substantiate your claim.) He will probably let you pass.

Once I was picked up in the town of Bude (its greater metropolitan area has a total population of 1,300) by the chief of police, who sent me over to Tyson's appliance store to see the mayor. I was terrified, but Mayor Tyson was reassuring.

"We just picked you up to see who you was," he told me.

After I told him who I was and who I fervently hoped to continue to be, he turned friendly and informed me that he and his entire administration were at my disposal. His town is near Natchez, where they have the classic revival mansions (the ones with the white pillars and the moss hanging from the pecan trees).

For a dollar a nice white lady of fading gentility will escort you around and show you how the "cupids on the genuine imported French chandelier correspond with the cupids on the imported Italian marble fireplace." I experienced some difficulty in keeping my attention on what she was showing me because I had just come from the office of the mayor, where I had been told that the town was an armed camp ready to go to civil war with itself at any time. (Subsequently, the war was declared with the mayor as one of the principal enemies. By the summer's end he had been bombed twice, but at this writing the poor man still survives, though in a shaken condition and with no lights left on in the window frames of his house.)

By the bye, don't rush around Natchez with your Zeiss-Ikon conspicuously slung around your neck in happy anticipation of the color transparencies you're going to take of the antebellum houses. We were stopped on the street by a policeman who told us all picture-snapping had to be cleared with the chief of police. He also warned us that it is a violation of Natchez law to go into anybody's house without phoning for an appointment first. Mostly it's the Negroes who don't have phones, but under the circumstances it's wise to be leery of any impulsive Southern hospitality that might come your way.

One more travel tip: when driving at night, don't throw lit cigarettes out the window of your automobile. If you do, it won't be Smoky the Bear who gets you. There's no way to tell the difference between your cigarette and a bomb fuse. Edgy Negroes, who are running short on churches, may let you have it with double-barreled shotguns.

The state very much wants tourist business. Consequently, tourist information centers and guide books are very common, but they omit mention of some sights the more adventuresome or curious tourist might like to see.

For example, they do not mention the Reverend R. Edwin King, a white native of Vicksburg who has an authentic Ku Klux Klan cross. He found it one morning in his front yard.

The cross was too heavy for its base, so it fell over and extinguished itself before much of it burned. The Reverend King, who is a Methodist minister and an integration leader, keeps the cross in his tool shed. There is no charge for viewing it

Another sight you may want to catch is a sheriff's party trawling for various missing persons on the Father of the Waters. When I was last there, they found two in as many days, but the natives say the catch is usually not so plentiful.

Mississippi is very proud of its beautiful girls, often referred to as "our angel-haired, blue-eyed darlings." In Vicksburg I saw a lot of them at a preliminary Miss America beauty contest (they prefer to have it called a pageant).

Jeri Joyner, Miss Philadelphia (where the three civil rights workers were murdered), was there. She forgot to smile during the promenade in ballroom dress.

Miss Canton (where there have been bombings and church burnings), Miss Clarksdale (civil rights workers arrested and harassed), Miss Hattiesburg (rabbi beaten there), and Miss Franklin County (Klanland) were all there looking quite pretty. To win the contest, however, you must be more than beautiful. You must also be talented.

Many of the girls demonstrated they are accomplished baton twirlers, which is as big among the girls in Mississippi as football is among the men. The state also abounds in "schools of cosmetology," which may explain why some of the girls are so pretty. Even small-sized towns have them.

Mississippi's detractors say the schools of cosmetology have the same curriculum as the University of Mississippi at Oxford. This is not so. None of the cosmetological schools have intramural football.

You will also want to see the color photographs of the state's two Miss Americas enshrined with Mississippi's other most-honored citizen, the late Senator Theodore Bilbo, in the rotunda of the new state capitol, a magnificent edifice built and paid for by a railroad in lieu of taxes.

The old state capitol, now a museum, has some dust jackets from a few William Faulkner books. The volumes themselves, I am given to understand, are banned in much of the state as injurious to morals and patriotism. The same building also contains Confederate Army uniforms, an educational display about the cotton industry, and some dusty birds' nests.

Mississippi can be a special thrill for your kids if they're the kind that have always wanted to see for-real G-men in action. The kids can watch them guarding a civil rights rally or pinching a few of the local freckle-bellies for bashing in the head of some Harvard kid they (the freckle-bellies) caught trying to register a Negro to vote.

Your kids will have no trouble spotting a G-man. Tell the kids that the men who wear the revolvers and smile are the G-men. The children should be warned not to talk to the other men carrying guns. Another way to recognize a G-man is to "look for the stranger." In Mississippi there aren't many strangers, only civil rights workers (easily detected because they are usually being chased by the natives), newspapermen (easily detected because they are usually chasing after the civil rights workers and the natives), yourselves, and the G-men who are usually waiting for the natives to catch up with the civil rights workers.

Finding a place to eat can be a bit of a problem for the Mississippi tourist. The very best restaurant in Jackson will serve anybody, no questions asked, but it's expensive.

In a few restaurants that have complied with the Civil Rights Act, the proprietors are liable to treat the luckless Yankee customer with the same welcoming hospitality they used to lavish on Negroes. Once when I explained to a restaurant manager in Laurel that I was not responsible for the NAACP party in her dining room, I was told:

"The law says we got to be nice to them n-----s, but there ain't nothing in it about you."

Most restaurants just do not obey the new law. They avoid it by getting a state charter and turning themselves into private clubs. Sometimes the "club" is a subterfuge. In such cases, any white man can buy a membership card for $1.00 to $50.00. This adds to the price, but not to the quality of the meal.

Other restaurants actually do turn you down for membership. I was turned down by the membership committee of the Rotisserie, said to be Jackson's second best eating place.

At the Travel Inn at Greenwood, where they have a club so exclusive that we registered guests were not allowed to eat in it, they won't let you starve to death. You may either eat in your room or, as we did, sit in a corridor somewhere between the men's room and the kitchen.

When we pointed out that we were white, and complained that the various noises and odors associated with the two rooms would dull our appetites, the management put us in a private banquet room. It was a little large for our wants, and the tables with dirty dishes, half-empty highball glasses, and overflowing ashtrays not yet cleared from the last banquet were distracting, but we got through our meal anyhow.

Two Mississippi hotels have turned themselves into clubs. If the trend should continue, the tourist can always outfit himself with a sleeping bag and roost on the side of the highways. The snakes and the mosquitoes may make pests of themselves, but the tourist will have an unparalleled opportunity to watch the sheet-and-pillowcase crowd do their night riding.

In the old days, before they established the big new FBI office in Jackson, Mississippi tourism was more dangerous. Now, if you are an American citizen and you get into trouble, just call up "the Embassy," as the FBI office is called, and they'll do their best to extricate you.

AUGUST AND SEPTEMBER

Neshoba County *corps de ballet*—beyond and below the FBI drags the river for the murdered civil rights workers.

The Klan has also been known to blow up places that offend its members' temperance principles . . . as here.

Natchez . . . two views (above and opposite) of fire bombing. The building was mistaken by bomber for civil rights headquarters.

Negro pickup truck with shotgun pellet decoration.

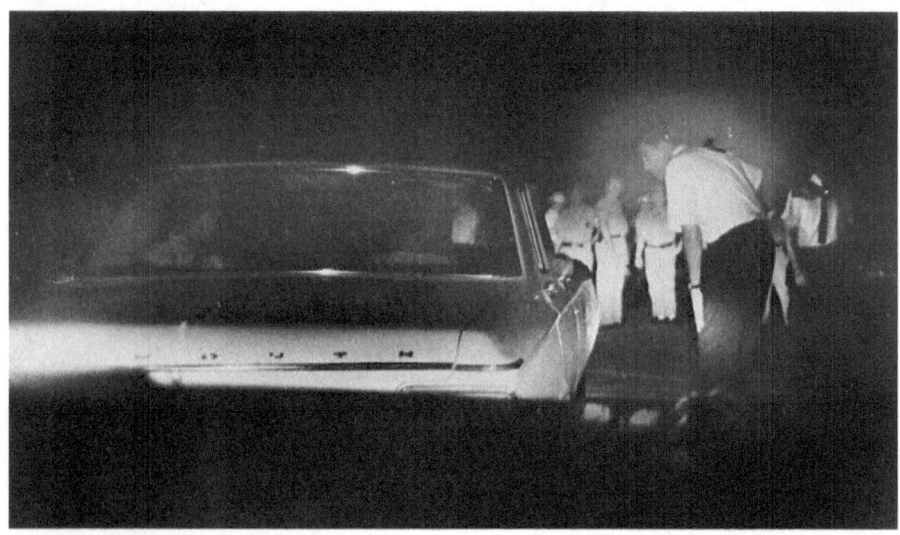

The Natchez police chief said, "This is still Mississippi. This is a segregated meeting. Don't get out of that car!"

At dusk in Harmony, Joe Greer guards his house.

Hartman Turnbow tells his neighbors what a national political convention is like.

"Pope John" at S. C. Williams's general store in Harmony.

Maxville, Attalca County: Reverend Watkins's congregation in rapt attention.

"Pope John" and the Cleveland mailman in the parking lot beside the church enlist support.

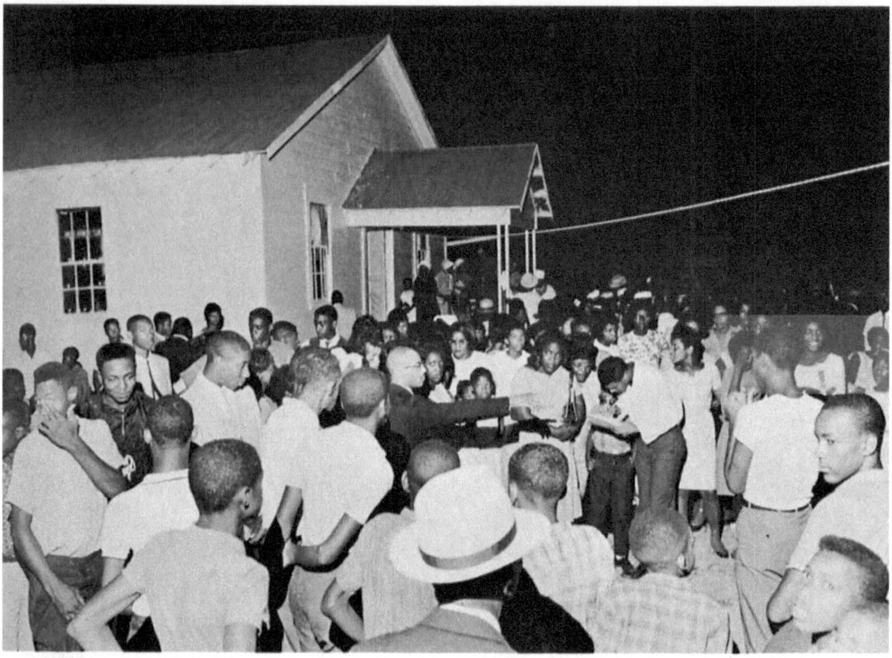

Outside Reverend Watkins's church the people sign up and join the movement.

Mileston, Holmes County: two summer volunteers at the general store after the "freedom meeting" in the church across the railroad tracks.

"... the first publicly announced, publicly held civil rights meeting that, so far as anybody could remember, Natchez ever had."

Mrs. Flowers in front of their new house, her husband's mausoleum in the background.

Roy Flowers's foreman, Big Lee, and a plantation overseer.

Natchez: The sweetly pretty girl with NAACP friends before the civil rights meeting.

Roy Flowers. An old man nearly eighty, he was waiting.

Orrick Metcalfe: "I'm tired and I can't fight anymore."

Malva and Carla Heffner . . . ready to depart for Jackson.

Carroll Oaks: the Heffners' last day. Red talks to his mother.

By night they guard.

The summer volunteers helped, too.

The night watch atop the community center at Harmony, Leake County.

By Labor Day the work is nearly done.

Harmony, Leake County: for the first time a few, at least, are in contact with well-educated people.

Negro farmers and their wives built the community center at Harmony, Leake County.

In Natchez many people live in antebellum houses: White—

—and Negro.

Greenwood workers on their way to the plantation.... "The cockleburs are the hardest."

Day's end—the bus takes the workers back to Greenwood.

Jerome Smith (with cane) and friends. "Nonviolence: an unnatural discipline on a natural response."

Lunch—a leg of fried chicken—for a worker on the Harmony center.

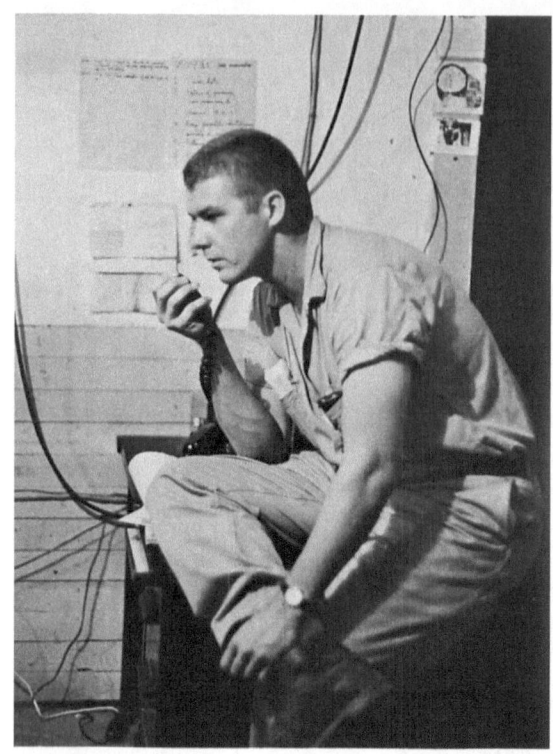

Mike Kenny calling TANGO from Greenwood.

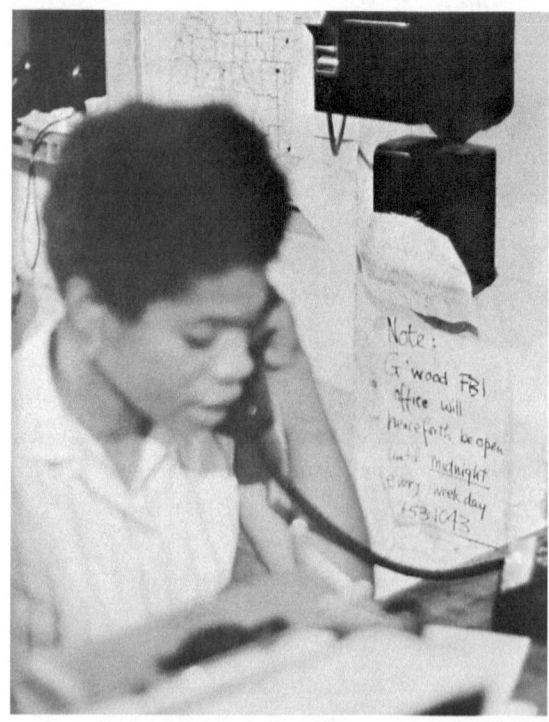

Nightly vigil in the Greenwood headquarters. Tall Janet from New York City on the phone to the FBI.

Greenwood's police commissioner.... "The civil rights workers scared the hell out of us."

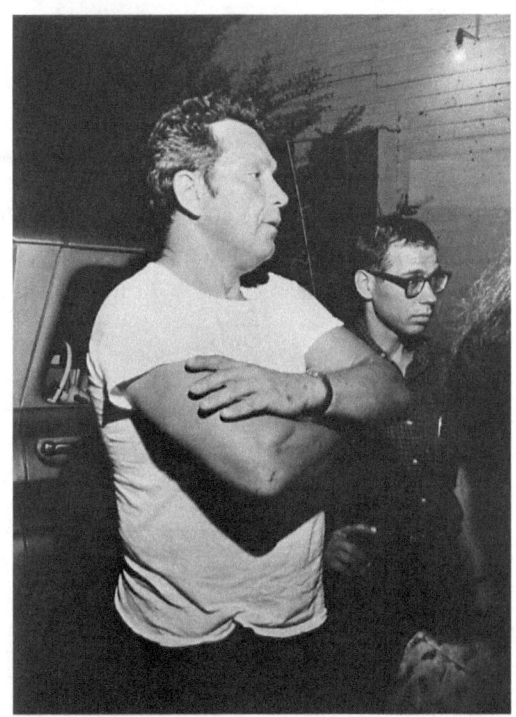

Abe Osheroff (arms crossed), the carpenter from Los Angeles.

Canton, Madison County. A deputy sheriff in his car in front of civil rights headquarters. He displays a photo that was arranged and taken by Mississippi law enforcement officers at Ole Miss during the federal occupation.

"THIS LITTLE LIGHT OF FREEDOM," sang tall Janet from New York City, "I'm gonna let it shine, I'm gonna let it shine, in the streets of Natchez."

She was on a street in Natchez as she bent downward, clapped the rhythm, and sang with careful enunciation for her listeners, a small group of raggedy Negro children. Janet's brown face lost the look of impatient anger customary to it as she imprinted the hope of liberty in the children's minds.

Standing a few feet behind her on the dead-end street, where the civil rights headquarters is, another young worker gave smilingly amiable support to Janet's intense rendition of the song. They had both driven into Natchez an hour or so before to take part in the first publicly announced, publicly held civil rights meeting that, so far as anybody could remember, Natchez had ever had.

It was not as it usually is before a meeting when the workers are too busy with last-minute arrangements for talk. Dusk was beginning to infiltrate this river town of ancient pastel-walled buildings, but the young civil rights organizers showed no signs of being off and doing.

A Negro townsman said, "It's too dangerous to move on the streets now. We've handed out one thousand leaflets. The people will come, or they won't. Anyway, they know we've dared to call the meeting."

The man was asked how many people would come to the meeting.

"At least five, not counting the workers, of course. We're hoping for more, but I'm sure we'll have at least five. Yeah, five, I'm sure of it," the man said, and added that he himself would be there, although he was tired from his day's work and being up all the night before standing guard with a friend who had gotten a bomb threat.

The building next to the headquarters had been bombed. It had been a bar and gambling place, but in the night the bomber crawling up the hill in the rear from the railroad tracks had mistaken it for the headquarters. It was gutted; only the facade was more or less intact.

George Green, the bullet dodger, leaned against a wall telling who in town would fix the cam on your car to make it go faster, or install a special switch so you could turn off your rear lights without turning off the front ones.

This was George's last night as a civil rights worker. He was going back to college, but Chico, his successor, would have to know these things.

"We're smothered. They won't let anything happen," a sweetly pretty girl told us as she took us around behind the headquarters and showed us their alarm system, a dubious assembly of wires and cans strung along the wall.

"Will you put this in the paper?" she wanted to know. "Will you send us a copy? They won't put anything we do in the paper here [the *Natchez Democrat*]. Nobody knows what's happening here.

"They put it in the paper that the Klan had a meeting last week. The police was out at Liberty Park directing the traffic.

"They won't be directing the traffic for us. They won't put it in the paper that we had a meeting. They won't let us have the meeting. I know it. I know it."

She pointed at the headquarters' two-way radio aerial, which had been bent double. "The police chief did it," she told us, "the night of the bombing when he saw they'd bombed the wrong house."

As the daylight dimmed into dusk, the fearful stories the youngsters tell about Natchez came to mind: the factory outside town that is supposed to be a distribution point for contraband automatic weapons; the woman whose son is supposed to have been murdered, but is too scared to talk about it; the two Negroes who are supposed to have been shot at a shopping center.

Before the meeting, they drove across the Mississippi River bridge to Vidalia, Louisiana, to eat in a Negro restaurant. They ordered shrimp-burgers, but everybody wanted a drink.

They ordered beer and Bloody Marys. Janet made tough wisecracks, and the workers who would be going to their posts in other parts of the state debated how to get out of town safely. Chico, who would be staying, talked about the young Southern-born civil rights workers.

"I feel badly for them. They're being passed up. They don't know as much as the kids coming down from the North with good educations. They can't do all the things the new kids can do, so they're not going up in the movement. It's too bad, because they were down here alone when nobody cared or knew."

The remedy, all agreed, was college. They told George Green, who was returning to college in Jackson, that he should go far away in the North, where the movement would not be close at hand to distract him.

"Anyway," one of them said, "the colleges in Mississippi aren't no good. What they gave [James] Meredith [first Negro graduate of the University of Mississippi] isn't worth more than a grammar-school certificate up North."

Abruptly they were ready for the meeting.

Everyone was given gum to take away the alcohol smell in case we were stopped by the police, and Henry Gill and I were instructed to follow close behind the young workers' Plymouth sedan.

Crossing back over the river in the night, we followed their car as they took an inconspicuous route to the meeting place, a field behind a school on the northeastern edge of the city.

Pine Ridge Road, the street leading to the field, was a confusion of Klansmen, Natchez police, police auxiliaries, Adams County deputy sheriffs, and irregulars of all sorts.

The Plymouth turned to go off into the field, but a police roadblock stopped it. It turned around to find another way in, but the second entrance was also blocked by police in full war regalia—helmets, shotguns, tear-gas guns. At a third turn off, the Plymouth was allowed into a parking area where several squads of police were deployed.

A man in a white shirt shined a flashlight inside the car, and the kids got out. We started to do the same, but the man in the white shirt was on us, saying he was the police chief.

He was in a rage, which gave his words a tremulous reedy sound:

"This is still Mississippi. This is a segregated meeting. Don't get out of that car."

We didn't.

But we tried to identify ourselves and talk to the man.

"Don't get out of that car. That's all I have to say to you," he told us as anger took his breath away and made his words gasps.

The youngsters walked into the night toward a dim source of light. The light went out. We sat in the car. The light went on again.

Another car came into the parking area. When the police flashed their lights in it we could see a Negro was driving. They waved it out of the parking area and it disappeared down Pine Ridge Road. The same thing happened three or four times, and we realized they were letting nobody but the workers onto the field.

The youngsters reappeared out of the night. They got into the Plymouth, and we followed them out of the parking area as the police followed us. By the third intersection we had lost the Plymouth in the traffic, and the police only had us to follow.

We cruised the night streets of Natchez for the better part of an hour to see what the cops would do. They followed, alternating between a motorcycle man and a squad car as our tail. Once we got out to make a phone call, but there were so many police in the alleys and around the corners that we thought better of the idea.

They followed us back to our rooms at the Holiday Inn, where thirty or more of them surrounded the place. It may have been the first time a besieged garrison had room service.

We ordered beer and sandwiches sent up, and from time to time Henry Gill poked his head out the door to see the chief of police skulking down the passageway. When he saw Henry looking at him, he jumped back around a corner.

After an hour or so he tired of the game and, raising his siege, led his army off for a night's rest.

The next morning we, in our turn, laid siege to his office, but gave up after he sent out word to us that he had said all he had to say the night before.

Mayor John Nosser was available, however. A short, gray-haired man, the mayor's semitic features confirm that he born in the Levant. He came to Mississippi as a young man, as did the many Lebanese people who settled mostly around Vicksburg and are about the only foreign language group in this insular and inbred state.

Nosser, who admits to being a moderate, has perhaps the best reputation of any elected official in the state. Even the civil rights people acknowledge he has struggled to muzzle the police and keep peace in his fearful and fearing city.

Having made his money in the grocery business, and come late to politics to repay the debt he feels he owes his adopted country, the little mayor has not learned to hide his emotions. That morning he was apologetic and upset.

His hands shook as he nervously and unsuccessfully lit and relit his pipe. His words tumbled out of his mouth in loud and agitated clusters:

"The chief of police is elected. That's the way it is. We have a weak mayor form of government. The only thing the mayor can do is use tact.

"I can advise. I can't order the chief to do anything. The man is elected by the people."

When it was suggested that his police department was little more than the Natchez Klavem (chapter) of the Ku Klux Klan, he demurred, but faintly.

One of the town's businessmen seconded the mayor in his opinions. Orrick Metcalfe is president of the Britton and Koontz National Bank and the head of a Chevrolet agency in Natchez.

A cultivated man who says he is a liberal by Mississippi standards, Metcalfe lives in an antebellum mansion called "The Parsonage," while his bank is housed in a nicely proportioned Doric-columned building that dates from the early 1830s.

"When I was on the board of aldermen I fought and fought and fought this for years and years," the banker said in commiseration with the mayor. "The civil service is protecting people on the police force they have no business protecting.

"I've fought electing a chief of police. I've fought for a city-manager form of government. I'm tired and I can't fight anymore.

"When you have ignorant people, you're going to have trouble. You're going to have a lot more killing. It's going to happen for sure."

We printed a story quoting the mayor and the banker. A few days later two of the mayor's family grocery stores and the banker's Chevrolet agency were hit by what the mayor called "sulfuric acid bombs." The damage was not great. (About forty-eight hours after this story appeared in the *Chicago Daily News* the mayor was bombed again—this time it was his home.)

A $5,000 reward for the bombers was offered, and the mayor said in the papers, "We do not know when, where, or whom the terrorists will strike next." But he told us he was sure they had been bombed in retaliation for what they had said in our newspaper story.

Ultimately there was a civil rights meeting in Natchez. It was at the same place, but earlier, before the sun had set, and the police didn't know about it.

Chico wept as he described what happened:

"It was beautiful. Thirteen people came. It started to rain, but they didn't leave. They said they'd come to the next one. Thirteen people. It was beautiful, beautiful."

What are the roots that clutch, what branches grow
Out of this stony rubbish? Son of man,
You cannot say, or guess, for you know only
A heap of broken images, where the sun beats,
And the dead tree gives no shelter, the cricket no relief,
And the dry stone no sound of water.
   —T. S. ELIOT, *THE WASTE LAND*

THERE ARE MOCK ORANGE TREES, wisteria, and mimosa in the Carroll Oaks subdivision of McComb, Mississippi, where the noiseless, subtropical air bespeaks not peace, but a hiding, spying intransigency.

Shannon Drive slopes and turns as it passes in front of the Heffners' white, single-level home. These new houses with the windows closed and the doors shut for the air conditioning always make it look as though their owners were away for the weekend.

The Heffners are home though. The larger of their two Chevrolets is parked near the yucca, a cactus-like plant in the front yard that resembles a miniature palm.

It's Malva who opens the door. She has no makeup on. Her dark hair has been left as it was tossed by the frightening night, and the glare from the morning's overcast sky picks up the vertical lines of tension and fatigue on her face.

"You know we're leaving. Today. We can't stay. We decided last night after what happened."

She guides us in and sits us down while she continues telling us what happened in richly accented words spoken rapidly but not shrilly. The training that Mississippi women of good family receive remains with her. Malva's posture is unconsciously perfect. She makes no awkward movement, and when she sits, sorting her correspondence and talking of her family's ruin, her body holds a graceful, womanly composure.

For weeks the town has been convinced that Malva Heffner and her husband, "Red," have been in collusion with the band of civil rights workers living in their headquarters across McComb, in the Negro district that they call Burgland Town.

"Last night was more than we could take. We were visited by these two students from a church organization—they had nothing to do with the civil rights movement—and this man from West Germany. They drove a Volkswagen with an Illinois license tag. I guess that's what did it, the Illinois license tag.

"The neighbors must have thought it belonged to some of the civil rights workers, because the next thing we knew the street was jammed with circling cars. I don't know what that German must have thought of America.

"He said it was just like it had been in his childhood under Hitler. We had to call up George Guy [the McComb chief of police] to get them escorted safely out of town. And George wouldn't have done it either, if we hadn't have told him that one of the three was a German."

She points to last night's uneaten supper of veal scaloppini as proof of the frame of mind her guests left in.

"I have one friend left who will invite me for coffee. I go over there, but every time I do, I'm afraid I'm harming her. Exactly four people from McComb have been in this house since the trouble started [six weeks before], and we did nothing, nothing."

She has been going through her papers making an inefficient attempt to pack, but now she stops to give full heed to her anger and sorrow for the town that has been her home for the past ten years.

"I nearly called up the civil rights headquarters to ask them, 'Will you send me over the biggest, blackest n----r you can find. I'm going to strip him, whip him, and make him sing Dixie while he crawls around a Confederate flag on the front lawn.' That's about the only way we can restore ourselves.

"Really and truly, we enjoyed and loved McComb. We still have a great many friends we wish well to. . . . I wouldn't believe it could happen, our being run out this way, if it weren't happening to us."

She goes silent for a moment, as if perhaps she is thinking of her childhood years in Scott County, or of her college days at Ole Miss ("I know it isn't much of a school, but the girls go there to get husbands, and it was fun").

Carla, her seventeen-year-old daughter, comes into the room. She's back only a few days from summer drama school in New York.

"It's breaking Carla's heart," her mother says after introducing us to the blond girl who favors her father in features but has Malva's sharp energy.

"This is her senior year in high school. She'll be missing all the activities, but if it weren't for Carla we would have gone stark, raving mad. She has her daddy's sense of humor."

"Oh really, Mother." The girl is annoyed at seeing Henry Gill and me. "I don't see why you have to put it in the papers. Why can't we just leave town without saying anything? What good will it do?"

Her mother tells her, "People have to know the truth, Carla, about how bad it really is."

"What if they know? Up North they'll read it in the morning paper, get mad over breakfast, and forget it. And the people in Jackson, with those newspapers there, aren't ever going to see it," the girl declares as she rummages through the kitchen looking for breakfast.

"My parents!" Carla cries out with youth's affectionate scorn. "I'm sure if these kids [the civil rights workers] hadn't come down here, they would have stayed in their shell. They never planned for this to happen.

"Before I went to New York this summer my parents told me not to join CORE or SNCC, and the next thing I know *they* had done what they told me not to do."

"We didn't," Malva replies, anxious to make it clear that the family had never joined any civil rights organization. "Your daddy just tried to see nobody got killed."

"We're being run out anyway," Carla replies. "Oh, I know we've got to go. There's nothing else we can do. I hope it's for the best."

Carla puts her choicest books, Brecht and Eliot, in a box. As she packs, she talks.

"My friends tried mighty hard to stick by me. I wouldn't ask them to jeopardize their houses and their cars."

Since her return from New York she has been the object of obscene telephone calls, the air was let out of her car tires while she was visiting a friend's house, and there was a real danger, particularly to the boys who had stuck by her, that they would be waylaid and beaten.

"I've had so much contact up in New York with people of different beliefs and races. I had a Negro teacher this summer. I just realized the differences between us and the Negroes are the differences in opportunities. We have them and the Negroes don't. I can't believe I'm better anymore."

Outside a car drives up with an orange U-Haul trailer behind it. It's Carla's father, Red.

Albert W. Heffner Jr. is the fifth of his line to be so named. He was born in Greenwood, where he was a classmate of Byron de le Beckwirth, the man accused of murdering the NAACP leader Medgar Evers.

However, you needn't know that to take Red for a Mississippi man. You can tell it by looking at him. His stance, feet apart, thumb hooked on his belt as he sips coffee, is pure Mississippi. So is his accent. But the furry warmth he imparts to it is his own.

While the women, and the Negro maid, Essie, put things in boxes, Red, whose hair has long since turned a blondish gray, gets out his diary to help his memory in recalling how it was that today his family is fleeing McComb for Jackson. A stout man of careful movement, he puts the diary down on the breakfast counter, pours himself coffee, pulls a cigarette out of his shirt pocket, and begins his story.

"Actually, it started back in the spring when the news was released about the coming civil rights 'invasion.' A group of people in the Carroll Oaks area [the Heffners were the first family to move into the subdivision in 1954] decided to form a neighborhood protective association.

"They were going to buy a horn to warn people in case demonstrators came into our neighborhood creating a disturbance, destroying property, or raping our wives, or so they told me. I thought it was sort of ridiculous ... like fallout shelters.

"I had no intention of being the sorehead. So I was willing to join, but my insurance business was keeping me pretty occupied and I just never got around to it." [In 1963 Heffner was "Life Salesman of the Year" for Lincoln National Life when he earned about $17,000.]

Red interrupts himself to show a set of instructions that the group, called Help, Inc., handed out to the residents. The rules say, among other things: "If trapped inside any particular room, flash light on and off repeatedly.... Follow instructions of block captain.... Be suspicious of all strangers until they prove themselves otherwise.... If desired, procure a tear-gas pencil or other automatic dispenser.... Be cautious, prepare yourself mentally and physically.... Temporary alarm to be three blasts from a shotgun or car horn."

Now Red turns to his diary. Sometimes he reads from it, and sometimes he merely uses it to refresh his memory as he speaks:

July 1
The real beginning of the long, hot summer ... three homes of Negroes have been bombed ... the son-in-law of a leading minister in the Negro community has been beaten ... efforts are being made to organize a neighborhood protective association.

Jan is in Monroe, Louisiana, for the Miss Louisiana Pageant. [Red's nineteen-year-old stepdaughter, Jan Nave, was Miss Mississippi, 1963–64. She was born one month after Malva's first husband was killed in action in Germany. Red and Malva were married a year later.]

Went to Clarksdale for friends' wedding.

July 2
Civil rights bill signed.

July 3
Had slight hangover but the wedding was beautiful. [Red chuckles as he reads that.]

July 7 (Back in McComb)
I wrote to Erie Johnston [director of the State Sovereignty Commission, the bureau of the state government responsible for keeping Mississippi free of United States domination]. *I asked Johnston to get the governor to make a statement in favor of law and order.*

There's lots of sentiment here that whoever did away with the three boys [civil rights workers murdered in June in Philadelphia] *are heroes.*

I spoke with two Negro leaders in an effort to establish a line of communication between the races... am concerned about the tension building up here in McComb.

Till this spring we always thought we had communication through our Negro teachers and ministers, but that's stopped now, and with our police system in a segregated society, we've had to depend on the informer.

[That Red should do these things is not out of character for him. He has always taken his responsibilities as a citizen very seriously. He is a past president of both the Pike County Little Theater and the State Multiple Sclerosis Association. He is a lay reader in the Episcopalian Church, and in 1952 was a leader of the Citizens for Eisenhower Committee. The McComb Chamber of Commerce gave Red its 1957 Community Service Award.]

My philosophy is that if you live in a town, you should contribute time and effort to the betterment of the town, not just take up space. This is Malva's attitude, too.

We worked for years to help build a youth center and a swimming pool on a "private funds-private club" basis so that there could be no question of integration.

July 10
At 3:55 a.m. a Negro leader called and told me that the civil rights headquarters had been bombed. Advised George Guy [chief of police] *of my Negro contacts and that I would keep him informed.*

July 11
Nothing of consequence.

July 12
Lazy day... didn't even make it to church.

July 13
Spoke with Oliver Emmerich [editor of the *McComb Enterprise-Journal*] *about setting up a meeting with the sheriff and some of the civil rights people. I didn't know any civil rights people at the time, but the situation was so touchy it seemed like a good idea.*

When I took Essie home, I drove by the house that had been bombed. In my innocence, this was the first time that I had even known exactly where it was located.

That evening, after a routine day, we were invited to our minister's home with several other local private citizens. It was then I met and saw, eyeball to eyeball, the first civil rights worker of my life.

He was the Reverend Don McCord, a white Disciples of Christ minister from the National Council of Churches. He is living at the bombed house.

[I stop Red to ask him if he is an integrationist.]

"I'm still not an integrationist. I see the logic of desegregation. It's been a personal opinion of mine that segregation is economically unsound, but that's one of the prices of living in Mississippi and you make it up in other ways."

July 14
Got a phone call from a friend in Washington. Told me that there is serious talk of moving troops in and putting Pike County under martial law. Said it seemed to Washington that all law enforcement had broken down.

Saw Reverend Wyatt Hunter of the First Baptist Church and Reverend Gault Robertson of the Presbyterian Church relative to having Don McCord speak to the men's clubs of these two churches. Both gentlemen politely, courteously, and firmly told me no, and said it was too volatile a subject.

I also advised the mayor [R. Gordon Burt Jr.] *about the Washington phone call.*

The same morning I went down and talked with Warren Wild, president of the Mechanics State Bank, about my call. I expressed concern that if I got involved with these people in any capacity that my business would go to hell. He pointed out that if troops were put on the streets of McComb that my business was gone anyway.

All my life I've been told that sooner or later everybody has to stand up and be counted, but they don't add that you should be prepared to stand alone.

Better part of the day was spent going to Hattiesburg working on a pension-plan prospect for my insurance business. You have to allow for the fact that we were still responsible citizens at the time.

That evening Don McCord called to ask if he could bring two or three other white civil rights workers to the house.

When they came, I showed one of the boys a letter from Carla up in New York. He cried as he read it.

[The letter says in part: "Last night I attended a SNCC rally for civil rights workers journeying to my state, Mississippi. As I sat listening to Mr. Forman, students from Mississippi, and others telling these people, 1,500 in number, about a vicious, almost-retarded-in-their-thinking group of people called Mississippians, I wanted so miserably to stand up and yell, 'No! No! You're Wrong!' But how could I do this? Mother . . . Daddy . . . they are right.

"I sat there as they told of life in Greenwood where I was born . . . and as they told of life in McComb where I live. I wonder how the Camelia City of America would feel knowing their public image is one of the most terrifying imaginable.

"And then I talked to kids who weren't much older than I. They were older though, and they were more frightened, and much braver than I have ever been. Here they were with a belief so strong, they were going 1,500 miles for it. It's so sad. I haven't been 15 minutes from it, and I could not do anything.

"But these kids were risking more than I ever had to lose.

"It's a privilege to live in McComb. Is it such a damn privilege to die there?"]

After the letter we discussed the interview Don McCord was going to have with the sheriff. Don was most hesitant about going alone to Magnolia [the county seat where the male citizens do close-order drill with rifles every Thursday night]. *I convinced him he would be safe, and promised that I would arrange my business to be in Magnolia that afternoon and follow him back so he wouldn't be isolated on the highway.*

In my naïveté I thought I was personally safe.

Malva and I convinced Don and the others that they had to get the Negro girls out of the headquarters where they were living under the same roof with boys of both races. Another thing we told them was that the white boys and the colored girls should not go to the supermarket together like they had been doing.

We hammered home the point that the kids should be neat in their appearance and not look like beatniks if they were hellbent on staying in McComb.

[The phone breaks into Red's narrative. It's his mother calling from Greenwood. "It's sad, but the community wanted no part of us," Red says into the speaker. "Mother, nobody made a mistake. That's the completely senseless part of the whole thing. . . . We tried to stay but this local vigilante committee's too much. . . . I meant it as a figure of speech, Mother. It's not really a vigilante committee. . . . Mother, I tried to stay in McComb to the bitter end. I know, I know, it's absolutely inconceivable, but it's happened."

As Red talks to his mother, Malva and Carla prepare to leave. There is no time to take the furniture. Only the most important things are going up to Jackson in the cars and the U-Haul trailer to the apartment the Heffners have rented, and from which they will be evicted as political undesirables after two nights.

Melva makes sure that Jan's Mississippi trophies and the family's treasure, the original shooting script for the movie, *Gone with the Wind*, are ready to go. As Carla takes Oliver, her parakeet, out the door, she defiantly says to the bird, "Guess we'll have to teach you how to sing 'We Shall Overcome.'"]

July 15
Don had his meeting with the sheriff. I followed him home and we had coffee and discussed what a good meeting it was.

July 16
Called the chief of police and told him about Don's meeting with the sheriff. Malva went by and had a chat with Oliver Emmerich. He advised her to be careful in view of the fact that our phone may be tapped.

July 17
Routine work day.
Malva invited our minister and his wife over for supper.

It was planned that Don McCord would come over after supper to discuss the projected meeting with the mayor and the police chief. There was a mix-up on the supper invitation. Our minister's wife had already started cooking supper.

Since we had extra food, I called Don McCord and asked him to bring one of the white boys and come over for supper. He brought Dennis Sweeney [a good-looking blond boy from Stanford University who had suffered a mild concussion in the bombing of the headquarters].

We ate hot tamales and made simple pleasantries until Carla called long distance from New York. We told Carla that Don and Dennis were here. We mentioned Dennis's name several times because Carla thought she had seen his picture in the newspapers in connection with the bombing.

A few minutes later the phone rang again. Malva answered. A woman's voice said, "Can I speak to Dennis Sweeney?"

Dennis got on the phone and the voice asked him how civil rights work was coming along. Dennis said he guessed all right, and then the voice wanted to know if he was a friend of ours.

Dennis asked the voice who it was, and the voice hung up.

That's how we knew our phone was being tapped or monitored. The only way the voice could have known that Dennis was at our house was by listening to the earlier conversation with Carla.

About ten minutes later a vice president of Help, Inc., called to say that people were getting upset about the strange car in front of our house and wanted to know whose it was. I didn't consider it any of his business, but being aware how touchy the town was, I told him exactly who it was and why they were there.

Now cars started circling our house. Dennis and Don began to get very nervous.

I phoned the FBI and told them what was happening, including our phone being tapped. The FBI said it could not be tapped because phone tapping is against the law. I replied, "So is church burning, and they've burnt nearly twenty of them this summer." [The actual figure is closer to thirty.]

It was agreed that our minister, who had arrived meanwhile, would follow Dennis and Don back to their headquarters. As we walked out to say goodbye I counted eight car loads of people watching our house.

We came back in the house and I got the pistol I had bought for Malva, but I couldn't find the magazine. We turned off all the lights and watched as some of the cars from the neighborhood which had followed Don and our minister came back to Carroll Oaks.

We called the FBI again and the police about the group that was still around the house. I'm glad I wasn't hotheaded enough to get my shotgun right then. I'm not trained in nonviolence.

July 18

Rumors went all over McComb.

George Guy came out and discussed the situation. George said that he couldn't protect us or he would be dead politically. [The police chief in McComb is elected.] George and I are pretty close friends, and I think he would have protected us if he could.

Went to bed about 1:30 or 2:00 a.m.

Malva woke me and told me to come into the kitchen. We looked out the kitchen window and saw cars parked up and down the street. We could tell there were people in them because we could see the glow from their cigarettes.

I got cussed by Malva because I opened the refrigerator door to get some buttermilk. The little light went on so that the people in the cars could tell we were up.

July 19

An FBI agent came out after church to discuss the phone calls.

We went out to the Holiday Inn to see an Olympic gymnast team work out. I went home to write some letters, but Malva stayed to swim.

While she was there the Holiday Inn manager, an old friend, told her that the Highway Patrol had told him that our house was scheduled to be bombed. We checked with the FBI and they said they knew about it and thought we did.

That night I kept Malva at the Holiday Inn. I came home and slept with a loaded pistol and shotgun. The civil rights headquarters wanted to send over some people to stand guard, but I said no.

July 20
Jan came home. She and Malva stayed at the Holiday Inn, where the FBI also stays. The manager asked them to stay in their rooms and not walk about the motel.

Continuous harassment calls.

Got registered letter from "Pooley" [McComb real estate man, Julius M. Alford] *asking me to vacate my office before August 1. I've known Pooley seven or eight years. He could have just phoned.*

July 21
Malva and Jan left for Vicksburg where Jan, as the reigning queen, has to preside over the picking of the new Miss Mississippi. Poor Jan, a has-been already.

[Mississippi girls from good families enter beauty contests. Winning is not remunerative. Red figures it cost him $4,000 last year to pay for expenses Jan incurred in connection with her ceremonial duties.]

During this period we estimate that we had over two hundred anonymous phone calls, although, and this is funny, we never had one on a Sunday.

Went to the Enterprise-Journal *office to discuss issuing a statement to explain that we had done absolutely nothing. The mayor was in the office, so we asked him if he would sit in and help us with the statement. He said no.*

[Mayor Burt has this to say about the affair:

"The community didn't take very kindly to what they did. The Heffners were more or less ostracized. We viewed them the way the Norwegians viewed the Quislings during World War II.

"The only way I could help them would be to implicate myself. The only thing I could have said was that the mayor said it was okay to have those people in their house, and then what a hell of a fix I would have been in.

"I didn't endorse that statement because I knew they'd collaborate with you know WHO."]

July 22
Picked up Jan's dresses for the pageant. Went to Vicksburg.

July 24 and 25
Pageant.

July 27
Back in McComb. More calls. The rumors are wilder by the day. One is that Carla is said to be dating a Negro in New York.
I realized that my insurance business was pretty well shot, and I began to look around for some new business possibilities.

Red closes his diary.

From July 27 to August 27, when Carla returned from New York, Red lost the fight to save his business. Red and Malva's families split over what happened, and although Jan visited a few times, she has lived with friends and relatives, many of whom drew away from Jan's mother and stepfather.

Red's money problems started to grow acute. He tried everything but he could do nothing to save his situation. Explanations and meetings helped no more than Red's diploma from Ole Miss.

The family's social life underwent a drastic change. Now they entertained FBI men. They became close friends with one who tickled them by referring to himself as "Stan, the Pollack."

Most of their other visitors were itinerant Northern doctors, lawyers, and teachers bold enough to venture into Pike County. They even had a visit from an Episcopalian bishop whose code name on their tapped telephone was "The Big Fisherman."

Around August 29, Falstaff, the family dachshund, and cats of the two other Carroll Oaks families who did not join Help, Inc., died. Apparently they were poisoned.

Red buried Falstaff in his backyard. Malva said he wept as he handled the shovel. In his diary he wrote: *"Did not believe it possible to become so attached to a little dog. He was about the finest little dog a family could have. He loved us all without asking anything but to be with us. Such love and loyalty is rare even in a dog."*

Now Red puts his diary in pocket. Everything is packed. He had put his house and country-club membership up for sale. He starts to go out the front door, remembers he has forgotten something, goes back inside the house, gets the electric coffeepot and his pistol.

A final look, and Red Heffner closes the front door, gets in his car, and slowly gears it into motion pulling the U-Haul trailer after him.

Aught's aught,
A figger's a figger,
All for the white man,
None for the n----r.
—MISSISSIPPI FOLK VERSE

AN OLD MAN, nearly eighty, he was waiting, sitting in his rocking chair, in his office across the dirt space from his cotton gin. He had his fedora on, the brim not snapped, doing his business of money, cotton, and Black field hands while he waited for us so he could tell us the story of what he'd done and all he owns.

When he came to Mattson in 1908 to work in the store for $25.00 a month and board, nobody around Clarksdale in Coahoma County knew the name Roy Flowers. Originally he wasn't a Delta man. He had come down from Cockrum, De Soto County, to work, and he hadn't known he was going to be so rich, and own everything, forty-nine square miles, the town, everything.

The liver spots on his face give his age away. Otherwise you wouldn't know how old he is, because his voice is soft and young, pleasing to hear when he talks about all he has, and how he owns it. When he dies, he will not leave it.

"I been here so long. I don't want to go back to my old home. That's why about ten years ago I went to New Orleans and picked me out a mausoleum. I had him come out and build me another just like it.

"I'll bet not more than 20 percent of the people know where they're going when they die. Lots of n-----s die in Chicago, and they have to ship them home here.

"My n-----s thought I was foolish, but it's smart to go ahead and be ready, and I just didn't want to be in the ground."

When he gets up from his rocking chair and with a young step guides you hospitably to his new home with the great cedar closets and the second-floor sitting room where the curtains don't have to be drawn because everything is air conditioned, you can see the mausoleum.

His mausoleum is marble, on his front lawn, next to his private church, with "Flowers" cut on it, and his two marble urns stand by the crypt door.

In life he is a joyful winner. Yet when he talks about his winnings in harmonious tones, it is not embarrassing to listen:

"I got four gins. I got controlling interest in the cotton seed oil mill in Tunica. I got the bank in Tutwiler. I got 7,000 acres in cotton. I got soybeans. I got some forest land, timber, I got more n-----s than anybody in Miss'ippi. I got more good land than anybody in Miss'ippi. I got the best business in Miss'ippi.

"This little town, Mattson, it's mine. I own it."

His hand, which does not tremble, offers us an envelope. Inside it are five promissory notes from five Mississippi banks, each promising to pay Roy Flowers $100,000 within a year. His hand extends another envelope. Inside it is a letter from a Memphis bank saying that Roy Flowers can have $750,000 any time he wants it—without security.

But money, even the three-quarters of a million he has on demand deposit for emergencies, is paper and ink writing. It's not land.

"I couldn't tell you how I got all this land myself. When people was losing their plantations they came to me 'cause I paid more money. I own all this land, all the land from here to Tutwiler.

"Someone asked me years ago to what did I give credit for my success. I told him, 'To the good Lord and Mr. Peacock.'

"Mr. Peacock—he was the president of the Clarksdale bank—would loan me the money to make the first payment. I'd buy the land for ten years' payments, and pay it before it came due.

"I got most of the land in 1930s. I couldn't make any money in those days, but the land was so cheap. I tried to get Mr. Peacock to buy some, but he was scared.

"All the banks were closing, but his stayed open, and I had faith in this country. Franklin Roosevelt, he put a support under the price of cotton, and we plowed up some cotton and he paid us for it. I'm the largest cotton grower in Miss'ippi.

"There's lots of good land in this country. There's good land in Ohio. Made a trip through there. We didn't care about expenses. We said the best and we had the best.

"They have good roads there . . . four lanes . . . I asked them how big their plantations are. They told me they didn't have plantations. They have farms. They're smaller, but that's good land too they have in Ohio."

We had Southern food for lunch, fried chicken, seasoned sausage patties, flat little biscuits, and beans. Beforehand everyone had a drink, and the women, Flower's wife, his sister-in-law, and Mrs. Jones, a houseguest from Moon Lake Plantation near Lula, told about how they have big parties at each others' houses in the Delta, and how it once was with five-cent cotton.

They are very kind, proud of their open hospitality and edgy lest the strangers from the North go away not understanding that the Delta is a good life, and the Delta people are a good people.

Miz Mary, the old man's sister-in-law, had misgivings, but while he rested after lunch she took us in her car to see some of the Negro people in the cabins, as she called the shacks they live in.

"Mack, these gentlemen are from Chicago. They're not Freedom Riders," she said by way of introducing us to a big, ugly old man who sat on a porch.

"What's all this about?" the tough old Negro asked, peeved at the interruption of his summer afternoon doze.

"Tell the men, Mack," Miz Mary said, "you're free to and go, aren't you?"

"I ain't gonna leave as long as you don't make me," the old man gruffed and would say no more than noises even for Miz Mary.

Miz Mary took us to Mattie's next, a cabin in better repair, with bachelor buttons, okra, spinach, and yellow old maids in the front garden.

"Have we ever beaten you, Mattie?"

"No, Miz Mary, I have never been beaten by nobody," Mattie replies, but the old woman prefers to talk about her son and her two "grans" (grandchildren).

As Miz Mary drives the car on the dirt road between the cotton fields to the next stop, she explains that the Negro families live rent-free, are given free wood for fuel, all the land they want to raise vegetables for themselves, and "we keep a car and a driver ready to take them to the charity hospital at Vicksburg."

Fannie was picking cotton near the side of the road. She is thin, as though she had worked all the fat off herself. Her brown Negro features under the round, straw sun hat and the squiggly pigtail coming out from under it make her look like a coolie.

"I'm old, really old," Fannie moaned. "I just sent in for my birth record to see how old I was. I'm around sixty-two or sixty-three.... Old, really old. I made my first cotton crop here in 1924. I'm not much at it now. I'm too old."

"Fannie, stop chewing your gum. Take your hat off," Miz Mary told her. "Tell them how you've been to Chicago, Fannie."

Fannie did, explaining that her three children lived on the city's West Side. "I don't do anything but babysit when I'm there."

"Do you write them about how bad we treat you, Fannie?"

"There ain't but one bad thing I write and that's when I'm sick."

"Do we whip you?"

"I ain't been whipped yet. They don't tell me get up and go to work or to get off the porch. When I heard my children were coming to visit, I asked Miz Mary, 'Is there any danger?'"

"Fannie and her children are always welcome here," Miz Mary says.

"There's an old blind woman sittin' down there in that cabin," Fannie points to it, "and ain't nobody gonna driver her away."

"That's right, Fannie. They can all stay as long as they obey."

Miz Mary begins to ease the car down the road toward the old man's house, but Fannie's shout stops her.

"Miz Mary, I hates to make a doctor bill just for a head cold. You got anything for it?"

"Yes, come up to the house later," Miz Mary says, and the car moves off.

Before the old man took us on a drive around the plantation, "where you can go all day and never leave my land," we met Big Lee. Big Lee, who is so big he is awesome, came into the breakfast room and stood in his bib overalls as the old man sat in a chair and talked to him.

"Big Lee, how do we treat ya?"

"It ain't what the rackets out [it isn't what people are saying]. I been to Chicago. I got children there. I can't stand it. I likes it here fine."

"Big Lee don't have nothing to do with civil rights," the old man remarked.

"That's right. I don't fool with it."

"You want to live in Chicago, Lee?"

"I wouldn't last long in Chicago. You have to bar the doors and windows like you're in a jail."

"We beat you, Big Lee?"

"Nowzah."

"We treat you good, Big Lee?"

"Yowzah."

"That's right," the old man said gently. "He don't want for anything."

"I don't want for anything, but I asked for it, and I gets it," Lee agreed.

"Ever been mean to you here in Miss'ippi, Big Lee?"

"There hadn't been a law that bothered me. I stayed in my place and they stayed in theirs. It looks to me like the n-----s are fighting more in Chicago and New York than here," this boulder of a Black man observed as the conversation ended.

"They're happy. We're happy. Everybody's happy here," the old man said as he led us off to the car.

He drove slowly so that we could see everything, and he talked as he drove:

"There's lots of my n-----s over there [as we passed a field where perhaps twenty people, mothers, fathers, and children, were picking cotton]. Here's a good cypress break. I could sell that cypress break for $40,000. I handpick half my cotton.

"During cotton picking a family'll make $40.00 or $50.00 a week, a lot of money for a n----r family. [Cotton picking time and cotton chopping time, which is earlier in the summer, are the two periods in the year when many Negro plantation families have cash income.]

"Ten or fifteen years ago I farmed with mules. It was nice to see them out in the field plowing. I had 400 mules easy. Started farming in 1916 on Castor Bow [bayou].

"See, see where that smoke is? I'm cleaning up that woodland for beans. All that land is mine. . . . See the wood behind those cabins . . . see all my n-----s get wood for the winter. . . . I don't know how much I'll make on that cotton . . . send my n-----s to the charity hospital at Vicksburg . . . it don't cost us so much. . . .

"I got a n----r church on every plantation [the Flowers' holdings are subdivided into twelve plantations]. N-----s love to go to church. I have a store on all my places. I don't run 'em. I rent 'em. It's nice for my n-----s . . . I don't see how I got ahold of all this land . . . finest land in the world . . . that cotton there will make [blossom into bolls] soon now . . . I just can't tell you what it's worth. . . ."

We stopped the car in front of a white frame building that is half-store, half-home. A middle-aged man with skin the color of light coffee comes out.

"That's Ezell Johnson," the old man told us. "He's my chauffeur. This winter we're going to the Breakers Hotel in Palm Beach, Florida, and Ezell'll drive. He's a smart n----r, too."

Ezell walked up to the car and waited for Flowers to speak.

"Ezell, I told these men, my people don't pay no attention to civil rights. None of them go to these meetings."

Ezell shook his head in agreement.

"I told them I got one thousand n-----s."

"Sen'tor Jim Eastland say last week you got over ten thousand. You got five hundred right on this place [one of the twelve plantations]."

The old man doubts the number is that high, says goodbye to Ezell, and drives to another spot so that we can take pictures of the people in the heat, standing on the crusty earth pulling the cotton bolls off the plant, and putting them into long bags, which they drag down the rows as they pick.

He watches:

"N-----s is funny things. I can't hardly understand how they can take the heat. They made me rich.

"Last year I lent 600 or 700 n-----s to Jim Eastland for a week to help him clean out his cotton—it takes money to handle n-----s. I give 'em Christmas money, let 'em sign up for commodities.

"Lots of people haven't got tractor drivers, much less day hands . . . now see how clean my cotton is. That's cause I got lots of n-----s. . . . Down there by Jackson, they burned a lot of n----r churches . . . that's foolishness. I hate to hear about that. I'll never have trouble with my n-----s because I'm good to them.

"See the cotton I got open? I got lots of it open . . . see those blooms? They're all open . . . I've been doing this all my life. I been lucky . . . I can drive off my plantation and I can tell the difference in plantations without knowing where I am. Those other plantations, they have no houses, no n-----s, and they have Johnson grass growing in the fields between the rows of cotton.

"Look at the n-----s out there. I suspect Ezell's right. I got two thousand n-----s instead of one thousand. Just look out there and see that cotton makin'."

"KUY1106, Greenwood base, calling KUY1106, Tango base . . . KUY1106, Greenwood base, calling Tango base."

Mike Kenny, a heavy-boned, fleshy blond graduate student in political science, sits on the edge of a table in the Greenwood civil rights headquarters and shouts into a radio transmitter.

"KUY1106, Greenwood base, calling Tango. Come in Tango, come in."

Loud static.

Then through the static a voice:

"KUY1106, Greenwood base, this is Ruleville base. Do you read me, Greenwood base?"

"We read you, Ruleville," Mike says. "Where is the cow? Where is the cow?" He is asking a coded question in order to make sure the voice coming through the receiver is the civil rights headquarters in Ruleville and not an impostor.

"The cow is in the barn," Ruleville replies.

Janet is a few feet away at a desk talking into the phone.

"Hell," she tells Mike.

The tall young Negro woman is waiting for an FBI man to come to the other end of the phone.

"Hell," she repeats. "There's no time to verify them. Anyway the code has been stolen."

Mike nods and says into the radio speaker:

"Ruleville, we can't raise Tango [the code name for civil rights headquarters in a town near Ruleville]. Try to raise them. You're closer than we are. Ask Tango if Margaret is there. Tell her, if she is, to get to a phone and call Greenwood immediately."

Ruleville repeats Mike's message to make sure it has it right.

Mike continues talking:

"She called from Webb [another town] an hour ago. Said there were two truckloads of armed white men outside the house and more coming on foot. Do you read me, Ruleville?"

He bends forward to listen to the receiver. Instead of a reply from Ruleville the radio gives forth a sequence of honking, quacking duck calls. Then there is laughter, and more duck calls.

Mike swears and says, "They're jamming us again."

Janet nods and says to the FBI agent on phone, "They're jamming us again. Why don't you or the FCC [Federal Communications Commission] make them stop?

"Look, can you get somebody up to Webb fast before one of our people is hurt? . . . Yes, she called an hour ago. . . . That's right, two truckloads of them. . . . No, I don't know Margaret's phone number. She just said, 'I gotta go' and hung up before we could get it."

Mike is back on the radio trying to break through the duck calls. Janet argues with the FBI as young people on the other office phones call around the state for help and information.

Someone comes into the headquarters of scratched old desks and makeshift shelves to say a fast, radio-equipped car is gassed up and ready for the run to Tango if need be.

This is not the first such night in Greenwood, but the young people do not grow accustomed to the worry and the waiting.

Miles to the southeast, Negro teenagers are playing cards in the dim electric light outside S. O. Williams's general store at Harmony.

The Reverend John Peck from New York City is trying to get them to throw in their hands and get in several waiting automobiles.

"Come on, you guys," he says. "If we don't get moving, we'll miss the meeting."

"Just let us finish the hand, 'Pope John,'" one of the card players retorts.

The white minister from Harvard Divinity School and Union Theological Seminary has been nicknamed "Pope John XXIII" by his youthful Negro friends in Mississippi.

Another figure comes out of the darkness into the dull light around the store and tells the teenagers to get a move on. A card player looks at the new arrival and says, "Those federal pants you're wearing won't save you."

The figure is indeed wearing an old pair of mailman's pants. He is a mailman on vacation from Cleveland, and, like the minister, has only been in the state a few weeks, but that has been time enough for the first fear to wear off and be replaced by an outward-going enthusiasm.

It is, he says, the only time in his life he has been able to do something important, and in his pocket he carries a letter to Cleveland asking for a year's leave of absence from the post office.

"I'll miss that $460 a month though," he says, his red shirt vivid against his black skin even in the poor light.

While the card players are cajoled into giving up their game and getting into the cars, a blond girl from the University of Iowa, whose father is a merchandise manager for Sears, Roebuck back home, drinks Coke and watches. She has been here most of the summer and says, "I'm going to stay until my money runs out."

She talks about herself, her family, and the movement:

"My father didn't approve of my coming. He believes strongly in property rights over human rights. He's a good man, the kind that says some of his best friends are Negroes."

She is a Catholic and says she got into civil rights through her membership in the Catholic Interracial Conference.

"I didn't get much support from my friends. One of my roommates at school joined the Peace Corps. . . . Now that we've proven ourselves, that we're not just coming for adventure, it'll get more support, even from the frats and sororities.

"They don't like to do something unless it's cool, but I think next summer the project will really draw the Greeks.

"The whole movement is changing. I hate to see it turned into a bureaucracy. The kids with better educations, white kids mostly, are taking over. Some of the Negro kids are pretty bitter about it. Don't blame them. This is more efficient, I suppose, but I hate to see it anyway."

Everyone is loaded into the cars, which bump onto the pitted road. Dust clouds the headlight beams and reflects the light back on the drivers following the first car.

The cars turn onto the paved highway outside of Harmony, and pick up speed driving west until they hit the Natchez Trace, where they turn north toward Attala County.

They probably would not have been allowed to go if one of the more experienced workers had been around. The mailman and "Pope John" don't have seven weeks' time in Mississippi between them, and they are leading an expedition into a county that has a reputation as a dangerous place.

The movement has no organization in Attala County and few contacts there. It has none in Maxville, a country community so small it isn't in the Rand McNally index. It is to Maxville the group is heading, to a Negro revival meeting there.

"Pope John" had happened on the revival the previous night, when he had tried to enter the country church to preach civil rights and had been refused by the minister.

The cars turn off the Trace and down several roads until they come to a clearing where there are cars and pickup trucks parked next to the old church where the revival is going on inside. The young people drive into the parking area, but are too inexperienced to park the cars so they can make a fast getaway.

The youths, in their late teens and early twenties, get out of the cars and go to the church windows, where they whisper to their peers within who are soon seeping out to join the partisans outside. There they are told what's up and help in the work of luring others into the parking area.

The mailman and "Pope John" talk to perhaps thirty more who have now come out and ask them to get the rest of the congregation, which may number another one hundred and fifty. Soon there are enough outside for a direct assault.

Robert, who is eighteen, goes to the side door, where he is met by the stout pastor, Reverend Watkins, who tells him, "We're having a revival meeting here tonight, boy."

Robert: "We just want to talk to the people."

Rev. Watkins: "We're having a revival."

Robert: "We're not going to disrupt the meeting."

Rev. Watkins: "That's what you're doing."

Robert: "If we were going to tell them to go junking and drinking, it would be a different thing."

Rev. Watkins: "I'm the pastor of this church."
Robert: "The people ought to have a say-so about us speaking."
Rev. Watkins: "This is for the pastor to decide."
Robert: "If you're leading your people into blindness—"
Rev. Watkins: "You saying I'm leading my people into blindness?"
Robert: "I didn't say that . . ."
Rev. Watkins: "I'm telling them everything I can afford to tell them."

As the pastor leaves and goes to his pulpit, a member of the congregation softly explains in the dark that Reverend Watkins and some of the others are afraid that the white people will find out that freedom workers have been in the church. So many churches have been bombed and burned.

Inside, the minister, whose dark skin looks almost gray in the sickly blue neon used to light the church, tells his now badly depleted congregation:

"We love everybody coming into the state [meaning the civil rights workers], but there is a time for all things. Tonight we feel responsible for you. Say Amen. [A few do, but without gusto.]

"I'll give the word at the right time, but we're in a church service. The pastor knows when the right time is because he is the pastor. Say Amen." [Seven or eight scattered "amens" come from the older sisters while the rest wait to be dismissed.]

Now the whole congregation comes outside and, with a little shepherding from the civil rights workers, forms a semicircle around the mailman who stands on an automobile hood. The mailman talks without polish but with much energy:

"Remember this ugly face," he begins, introducing himself and "Pope John." "We're not here to harm anyone. We're here to help and we're all Americans.

"The government is with us. The Department of Justice is with us. We're here to help you help yourselves in your communities. . . . We in the North aren't free, but we have the vote and we want to be free.

"If you want something, you have to organize and struggle. I don't mind leaving my blood in Mississippi for my cause. Now, are you satisfied with the system, or do you want a change?"

A number say they want a change.

"Do you realize how powerful the vote is? If you had the vote, you wouldn't have a Governor Johnson or a Sheriff Rainey [Lawrence Rainey, sheriff of Neshoba County, where the three civil rights workers were murdered].

"Do you want to make $2.00 for picking one hundred pounds of cotton?"

"No," is the murmured reply.

"Are you afraid?"

"No," again.

"What do you want?"

"Freedom," many of them say, but few shout.

"How many men can I get to be our guides? We don't know Attala County. We need housing for our workers. We have no place to live but your homes. Don't put yourself out for us. If you eat peas, we eat peas.

"We need a central place for an office. Remember, all we do is set the groundwork for your organization, then you take over.

"This is for you. I can get back on a Delta Airlines plane to Cleveland whenever I want."

Paper is passed among the people so that those who will help as the mailman asked can sign their names and where they live. Many of the people sign.

In Greenwood, some of the white civil rights workers are drinking beer in a Negro restaurant. They talk about making sure that hate does not capture the feelings of the people in the movement. They speak of what they call "the beloved society" in which all men will be reconciled.

A few blocks away at headquarters a voice says, "KUY1106, Greenwood base, calling KUY1106, Tango. Come in Tango, come in."

The radio's loudspeaker answers:

"Honk, honk, quack, quack."

ALTHOUGH THE HALF MOON was bright over Leake County's rough central Mississippi countryside, it was hard to see the boy because his skin was dark. You could make him out, though, standing by the nearly finished oblong building, holding a shotgun.

Guard duty bored him. He put the gun barrel to his lips and blew across the opening, making the same low-pitched vibration that comes from blowing across the top of an empty soda pop bottle.

"You're gonna kill yerself," an older boy told him and took the gun away.

The wooden structure they were guarding is a community center that the people of Harmony had built this summer when the whites said they could not use the abandoned Rosenwald school building for their Freedom School.

Mississippi has many Rosenwald schools, so named because much of the money for the first Negro public schools in the state came from Chicago philanthropist Julius Rosenwald.

The community center stands near S. O. Williams's general store with the gas pumps in front. The two buildings face a rutted crossroads that is impassable after a rain. This is the center of Harmony, a few miles outside of Carthage, the county seat, which didn't get a railroad until 1928.

It's in places like Harmony that the idea of nonviolent resistance is passing fastest. During the summer, whites burned a cross in a field not far from the crossroads, and several houses were shot into. Now, unlike times past, the Negro farmers are responding by arming themselves.

Joe Greer, a light tan man with forty acres of land and a hospitable wife, Alice, who does most of the talking, sits by night hidden in back of his farmhouse with pistol and rifle when things are tense. So many of Joe Greer's yeomen-like neighbors do the same that it is dangerous to drive off the paved highway into the Harmony area after sundown if your car is unfamiliar there.

In the days before the school at Carthage was to be integrated, the Negroes' apprehension and armed vigilance increased, but even where there was no federal court order, and no suspense about the outcome of the opening day of school, Negroes were carrying guns.

You could see the guns on the front seats of cars as people drove to night civil rights meetings in Mileston in the Delta. The Negro people in McComb will tell you that they are armed and ready to throw up roadblocks in their section of the town against the police and the Klan if trouble starts. (Subsequent to the appearance of this story in the *Chicago Daily News*, McComb Negroes did indeed barricade the streets against the police.)

Even the civil rights workers are uncertain about nonviolence. In some places they have stopped preaching it, and are urging the contrary.

Jerome Smith, a long-limbed man in his late twenties, sat on the edge of the Greers' porch one morning poking at the dirt in the garden with a cane he uses to support a bad leg. He was in charge of civil rights activities in the Leake County area, and had dropped in on Harmony to talk about the upcoming school integration.

He was talking with five or six younger workers about finding some parents who would dare to send their first-grade children to the white school, but the conversation had wandered off the topic to the question of violence and nonviolence:

"This country discouraged nonviolence. There was a real loss of faith in it by Negroes after Medgar and Chaney [James Chaney, one of the three civil rights workers murdered in near-by Neshoba County] were murdered.

"Very few of us accept nonviolence as a way of life. It's an unnatural discipline on a natural response.

"We were willing to accept it as a tactic as long as it was sanity, but it's just not sanity to give your life away. Now it's not a question of violence and nonviolence, but one of survival. If it comes to that [violence in self-defense], we may lose support from the outside."

The subject temporarily played out, he turned to a symmetrically featured young man whose skin is a shade lighter than his. This is Theobis. Until eighteen months before, Theobis had led a somewhat uncertain but ordinary life as a factory worker in Canton.

Theobis's civil rights agitation eventually cost him his job in the can-opener factory where he polished handles. He became a full-time staff worker and progressed in the movement until he was put in charge of the work at Harmony. He lives with the Greers, and on that day his main preoccupation was finding children to integrate the school.

Jerome Smith warned Theobis:

"We'll have to play it tight, real tight. We can't afford to irritate the people [who have promised to send their children], but try to pin them down. Try to pin them down to which cars will carry them up there and which people will go. You'll have to sneak by the houses of the people that are shaky about it."

Inside the farmhouse, Mrs. Greer talked about the situation. She said she would send a child if she had one of school age, but she is less fearful than most. She and her sister were among the first to run the gantlet of registering to vote:

"It took me two years to register to vote. Then, when we went to vote, they didn't put the ballot in the box. They put mine to one side.

"My sister said, 'No, I'll put my ballot in the box myself.' They told her the law was that she had to give the ballot to them.

"She said, 'What law? Mississippi law?' Then they said if she didn't give them the ballot she couldn't vote.

"Not long after, the man at the gas station told Joe, 'Don't you know you're fixing to get your family killed?' Sometimes on weekends [when things are usually roughest] he don't take off his clothes for being out back watching all night. But he told the high sheriff [old English expression still used in some rural areas of Mississippi], 'I'm gonna protect my home.'"

Down from the Greers on the roller-coaster trench through the hills that serves as a road, a trim-looking Negro farmer in a khaki cap and an orange shirt is having a soft drink and talking about the upcoming school integration:

"The main thing about white folks is you can't depend on their word. They'll tell you one thing and do another. I'll be frank with you. I'm afraid. I'd send one of my other kids, but that's my baby. I couldn't do it."

The federal court order stipulates that integration is to be done a grade a year starting with the first grade.

"They're against the Negroes all the way. If it were me going to the school, I'd go in a minute. I'm not afraid of them at all, but I just couldn't risk my baby.

"I hope somebody does send their kid, though."

S. O. Williams—his color is that of lightly stained wood—listened to the farmer but said nothing. Williams, who owns the general store, is suspected by the APWR crowd of being rich. Even reputable whites, like George Keith, the newspaper editor in Carthage, think Williams may be the wealthiest man—Black, white, or Indian—in Leake County.

Such talk worries Williams, and when he hears it, he denies he has so much money. Only the store and a good-sized farm, that's all he has, Williams will tell you. Those APWR's might resent a Negro who has too much money. They might fret about a rich Negro.

Williams has signed one civil rights petition, but although he says, "I'm for anything that will help the colored man progress," he feels caught in the middle:

"Before this came up, 40 percent of my business was whites, and not just peckerwoods [slang for white trash], but good whites. Before this came up, I don't know whether I had more white or colored friends. That was before the civil rights came up."

In town, the white people were hoping that no Negro children would be brought to the school on registration day.

They were resisting up and down the line, of way they knew. When the official national Little League said the baseball game had to be integrated, Carthage withdrew and started the Dixie League for the kids.

But that didn't sound so good for a county wanting to attract what they call "industrialists" to locate factories there. So they changed the name again, this time to Little Boys' Baseball, but kept it segregated. (Little Boys' Baseball can be found throughout the state.)

Under the pressure, the white people fell to suspecting each other and telling nasty stories on each other. It got so bad that George Keith had to put a piece in the paper about it:

> Some of the tales told on the streets of Carthage this week ridiculous. Some are downright mean. To say that two of our most respected businessmen . . . have each made sizable contributions to the NAACP is about as absurd as starting the rumor that Reverend Martin Luther King has come to serve as interim pastor at the First Baptist Church of Carthage.
>
> The story even got out on this end of town that a lady . . . said that the Chamber of Commerce was sponsoring a boycott of white folks against white folks. . . .

The Chamber wasn't, but some of the white businessmen pressured into refusing service to Negro customers in Harmony. The butane gas man and the soft-drink bottler both have given up delivering out there.

Leake County had plenty of problems before civil rights boiled up.

It's hard for a white man to make a living on the hilly little farms, and people like the county agent, who want to help, don't seem to have much to help with. It's like the sign he has on the wall behind his desk:

The 4-way test of the things we think, say, or do:
1) Is it true?
2) Is it fair to all concerned?
3) Will it build good will and better friendships?
4) Will it be beneficial to all concerned?

For O. C. Allen, the little, bald farmer who must find a living off eighty acres of land, the "4 way test" doesn't make the perennial hard times easier. Like many of the farmers, O. C. does what they call in Leake County "public work." That is, he has an outside job.

To fill out his income he works as a school-bus driver, but many of the other farmers have to drive to a Jackson factory job every day.

"I started farming in this patch in 1926," O. C. said, looking down from his seat atop his golden orange tractor. "In those days we got as high as a bale of cotton an acre, but half a bale average, not like now when we get a bale and a half or two bales even. That's all since we got agriculture teachers and all that, and they taught us all different kinds of methods."

He took his hat off and wiped his forehead before continuing:

"They got Miss'ippi low-rated, but it's one of the most beloved states. Miss'ippians don't believe in no such stuff as killing folks. Our people are a Christian people.

"If it wasn't for my church and my Lord, I'd be the most miserable man on earth. I'm a Primitive Baptist, and I'm happy to announce it. Some's against us. They give us the name of 'hard-shell Baptist.'"

O. C. would prefer to talk about race and religion, but he is willing to answer questions about his farming:

"I can make a living at it, but not money. A man has to have a sideline like the school bus. Only two things I know, how to raise cotton and transport children.

"Can't make money in cotton. Labor's too hard to find, and puts me to too much trouble. I got some Choctaws that pick my cotton. Only trouble is I gotta get 'em and carry 'em back. I'm trying to work my way into beef cattle, more or less, but that takes money."

Then he went back to his pet subject:

"I met this colored brother. I told him, 'Don't think the white people will let you down as long as you stay the same, but when it comes to mixing, that's against God's law.'

"The way the situation's got now, I daren't invite him to preach in my church. Boy, I tell you, I'd be afraid to undertake that now. It's pitiful but they'd say I was in the NAACP.

"The ones that are going into this is the young, hot n-----s, not our good old Mississippi n-----s. These freedom workers are lowdown snakes in the weeds.

"Yeah, it's these young n-----s that cause the trouble. They want to get with the white women. But I say, 'What is will be and it shall come to pass, and the world will grow wickeder and wiser.' That's what I say."

On school integration day Carthage was on its best behavior. The town wanted to make a good impression. It had gone so far as to set up a press room for the visiting reporters, who were offered free cigars by a local politician who stood outside the door holding them in a paper bag.

Most of the morning nothing happened. No Negroes showed up. The press, the police, and town leaders looked at each other and tried to stay cool in the late summer heat.

A few minutes after a white shop clerk on the courthouse square said to a friend, "Goody, there's none come," an old car drove up to the police guarding the school.

Inside it was a six-year-old Negro girl.

She was registered without incident.

A few days later the NAACP reported the girl's father lost his job.

A few days after that a Negro church outside Carthage was fired.

I am Mississippi bred, I am Mississippi fed
—nothing but a poor Black boy;

I am a Mississippi slave; I will be buried in a Mississippi grave
—nothing but a poor Black boy.
 —ANONYMOUS THIRTEEN-YEAR-OLD
 "FREEDOM SCHOOL" STUDENT

4:30 A.M. ROUTE 82 and Avenue G in Greenwood.

The police went off duty a few minutes ago, and the few Negroes in the all-night 82 Grill seemed relaxed. Nobody is watching.

Outside it is still black night, but the cocks have begun to crow, and dogs, unseen, can be heard barking. A Negro drives up in an old black-and-white Chevy and a teenage boy with a sheer handkerchief tied over his hair shouts at him:

"Where you driving this morning, P. T.?"

"Ruleville," the man says.

"Ask Mr. Charlie [Negro term for white people, especially white bosses] if he needs a foreman," the boy asks laughingly.

"That's my job."

"You can tell the man *I* want a job sitting under a shade tree . . ."

5:00 a.m. The working day is beginning.

Solomon, a man of light brandy color who seems younger than his forty-one years, is starting his first day in a new business, that of picking up field hands from their houses and transporting them to the plantations in the surrounding countryside.

For this work he has just acquired a blue, freshly painted secondhand bus, which he hopes to pay for from the fifty cents he gets from the plantation owner for each laborer he is able to deliver daily.

Being new in the business, Solomon has not yet outfitted his bus with a barrel to carry drinking water to satisfy the thirst his passengers will develop in the fields under the sun. The other buses that move from spot to spot picking up workers in the Greenwood dawn have them lashed to little rear platforms.

Solomon knocks at the window of a rundown frame house. His rap is firm but not too obtrusive, as he says, "Ezra, this's Solomon. When you fixin' to come to work?"

A voice from within: "Be with ya tamoora . . .

Solomon accepts the answer. There is competition among the bus drivers for the fifty cents; the workers must be wooed to ride with him.

He gets back in his blue bus, drives down the street, and, as he turns the corner, a competitor passes him going the other way. At the next house he must wait, but his passenger, a limping man, does appear and walks slowly, with Solomon in the lead, from his house to the bus.

Solomon goes on, stopping in vain at some places, and with success at others as the people—women, children, and men—come out of their houses. Some move very slowly to get on the bus. None moves fast.

They look old and hurt, even the children, as though they had been bruised so that each step, each movement of the body, must be made with hesitation.

A mother sits up toward the front of Solomon's bus with her little boy beside her. She and the boy will make $4.00 today when they get to the plantation where they will work for ten hours weeding beans.

"The cockleburs are the hardest," she says, "but there's coffee weed and pig weed too."

She had brought food for herself and the boy, whom she hopes to send to East St. Louis, Illinois, where he can go to a good school. In the mother's paper sack there is bread and chicken necks. She and the boy will drink water and cola.

It has not been a good year, she says. "We haven't gotten but a few weeks work this year, but I hopes to get more pickin' cotton if they allows us to pick."

Mechanical pickers (they look like large, rubber-tired steel anteaters) are taking work away. Along all the highways of the Delta, from Yazoo City north, there are signs advertising PICK CLEANER COTTON-DEFOLIATE WITH FOLEX.

The Folex is sprayed from biplanes that have wires and struts between the wings. They look like war surplus from the Lafayette Escadrille. You can see them everywhere in the cotton counties of the Delta. The newspapermen call them the "Confederate Air Force."

The Folex makes the leaves drop off the cotton plants so the mechanical pickers can snatch up the white bolls without "green stain."

When Solomon has all the people he thinks he can entice on the bus his first day, he swings west and takes his passengers toward Indianola, where the plantation is.

10:30 a.m. Buff Hammond stands in front of his Greenwood cotton brokerage office. He is the police commissioner:

"The civil rights workers scared the hell out of us. We're not used to tension. Mississippi is only 42 percent colored, but it's 65 percent in the Delta. Here in Leflore County there's thirty-two thousand of them and only sixteen thousand of us.

"I'm not fooling myself; I know it isn't going away, but the Negroes are economically inferior, and morally inferior, and they're inferior in ambition.

"We're never going to accept it any more than you in the North have accepted integration. I been North. I know you don't accept it.

"The n-gras here are expressing what they always felt, I guess."

2:15 p.m. Ruleville. Between Indianola and Greenwood but north of both in Sunflower County.

Fannie Lou Hammer, a woman who can understand the mother on Solomon's bus and express it, sits on the porch of her house. She has a big pecan tree that she loves in the front yard.

"My mother lost her eyesight when she was hit [accidentally] with an ax while she was cutting down trees to clear a corn field," she says.

She looks right at you with warm eyes, but her large dark brown features seem worn with a passion that is too exhausting for her overweight frame.

"The first time I remember not being satisfied was when I was a small kid.

"My family picked sixty bales of cotton, but we had no shoes. The white people had shoes; we was workin'; they wasn't. They had food; we had none. Oh Lord, how I wished I was white."

The country first heard of her when she appeared on television at the Democratic National Convention, a reproving, accusing Black voice: "Righteousness exalts a nation, sin is a reproach."

They hate her in Mississippi. At the Carriage House, Natchez's best restaurant, a grand dowager of a white woman at the next table says of her: "That n----r woman from Ruleville is the best actress I've seen in years."

Over in Canton, Madison County, a deputy sheriff spits before saying, "Hell, that n----r wasn't never beaten the way she said on TV."

Neither hatred nor fame brings money. Her husband is unskilled and mostly unemployed:

"We women have no chance to be women here; our education is poor, but the men's is worse."

"My husband says when they were boys they had to be out with sticks knocking the cotton stalks instead of being in school. It was so cold that he'd put his feet where the cows would have been laying to get them warm."

Mississippi winters are cold, and the humidity gives the frosty air a rheumatic penetration. The poorer people's houses are built on the theory that the climate is always subtropical, so that in winter half of the people seem to have walking pneumonia.

She continues to talk, but is interrupted by a Confederate Air Force plane that drops low and buzzes her house. After it has passed on to the west, she says:

"They do it all the time. It don't make no mind. . . . If we can only hold on here. It has been better this summer, but I pity the Negro people of Mississippi when these students leave.

"These people are not here for no kind of social fling. They taught us things we never knew . . . Negro history. First time I learned about Frederick Douglass [Civil War–era Negro abolitionist and writer] was last September in *Ebony* magazine. There's nothing wrong about teaching us about us.

"We have a beautiful heritage. We are the onliest people that have had one man to march through a mob to go to school. We are the onliest people to have our babies sold from our breasts. . . ."

7:30 p.m. Greenwood civil rights headquarters.

Silas McGhee is a thin, tall twenty-one-year-old. The way he bends over and goes to pieces when he laughs makes you think he is younger than he is. Silas has none of an older person's caution about showing his emotions.

By nature, most of his emotions seem to be happy ones, as though he had a vocation for joy. He is lucky, too. The bullet left only a small scar on his cheek. The scar is about three shades lighter than his milk-chocolate complexion, but he has not been disfigured.

"The thing that really brought it about was people treating my mother so bad," he explains.

"She owned this little farm [fifty-eight acres] right on Highway 82. The [white] man joining her land started a subdivision—he kept asking her to sell, which she didn't do, so the next thing, the bank started to foreclose on her.

"She was sick [widowed since 1949], but my mother still didn't want to sell. She gets a lawyer [white] and he gets her to sign a deed of six acres of her land. That was to be insurance for him that she will pay him when it comes time. Then he goes right off and sells it to the man with the subdivision.

"They send a man out to stake off the six acres of my mother's land. She protests him, and he has her arrested. They take her down to the jailhouse, but they don't put her in. She went to court. [The case is not settled yet.]

"Then they arrested my brother Jake. My mother went to see him in the jailhouse and the cop pushed her so she pushed him back and they have her arrested again. [Silas's mother then fled to Jackson.]

"On the afternoon when the president signed the Civil Rights Bill I made up my mind to try the Leflore movie theater. I asked some friends if they wanted to go. At first they said they would, then when they saw the theater, they changed their minds and waited while I bought a ticket.

"I don't remember the movie. I didn't enjoy what I saw of it, mostly because I was thinking I'd have to go out of the theater. See, pretty soon somebody threw a paper cup at me.

"Then about two minutes later, a white boy hit my head with his elbow and another boy attempted to pour a soft drink on me. I stood up and asked them not to pour the drink on me.

"They didn't stop, so I went to the manager who said for me to go back and have a seat. The minute I took my seat about fifteen of them were gathered around me. One asked, 'What will it take for you to leave this movie?'

"I said to him I paid my dollar to come here and see the movie and I do not intend to leave until I've seen it. He told me, 'This ain't no n----r movie. If you care anything about your race you'll get up and leave. It'll look mighty damn bad for us to throw you out on the streets. Is you going to leave?'

"I said no.

"That's when they jumped on me and started hitting me. I pushed them out of the way and ran to the manager's office. I asked to use the phone. He told me no. I asked him again, and he still said no. Then he say I'll walk you around to the police station, which he did.

"I came away from the theater with a bruised nose and a couple of knots on my head. The cop looked at me sort of funny—he said I'll get in touch with you, but I never heard. . . .

"I went home and it was hurting and I was thinking next time I'll get someone to go with me who won't turn. I asked my brother Jake, and he said he would go. We did and the same thing happened at the theater.

"So we decided to get a larger group. This time we had Jake and my other brother Ben and three others from Greenwood . . . friends.

"We went in. After five minutes the manager asked us—he pleaded with us—begged us to leave.

"'I can't put you out of this movie. You have as much right as anybody else,' he say, 'but please, just for this night, please leave.'

"We told him we would leave, but we would be back. A few days later Jake and I and Clarence, my oldest brother [a soldier just back from Korea who was in uniform that day] went back to the movie. We enjoyed the picture, but I was worried about the crowd on the outside of the theater.

"After the movie we called a cab. They didn't bother us getting into it, but then the crowd started throwing stones and busted the glass in the cab window.

"The next time everything was okay until it was time to leave the theater. It was just Jake and I this time. We called three cab companies, but none came. So we called the civil rights headquarters.

"They got a Negro doctor to pick us up. His car windows were smashed, and Jake and I was cut by the broken glass, but the doctor wasn't hurt."

Silas says he likes exciting movies. He laughs instead of answering when you ask him if he has seen one more exciting than his own life.

"Next day I went down to the courthouse to try and register. Three men in a pickup truck got me and took me to a garage and beat me up. [The FBI subsequently arrested the men for violating the Civil Rights Act.]

"From then on every day I participated in demonstrations and voter-registration work. Then one day I was over in Baptist Town [a Negro section of Greenwood], parked on the wrong side of the street. The cop tells me to move and then he says, 'N----r, I'll pull your damn neck off. I'll get you later.'

"Later I was parked next to Lulu's Cafe on H Street. It was raining, so I decided to stay in the car until it stopped. That was the biggest mistake I made.

"I sort of dozed off and went to sleep. Next thing I knew I was shot in the head and was in the hospital."

Silas's favorite movie stars are Yul Brynner and Susan Hayward. His favorite picture is *The Ten Commandments*.

AFTERWORD

THE SUMMER IS OVER. Now there must be an asking of questions, and a summing up.

They came, hundreds of students, mostly white, and they did honor to their young manhood and young womanhood, but what did they accomplish?

Did they accomplish anything above showing that it is possible for a youth in good health to sustain a direct hit from a powerfully swung baseball bat on the back of the head? They did accomplish more, but it is difficult to say what, beyond that Mississippi will never be the same.

The Negroes still don't vote, yet it is a changed state.

Linda, a good-looking, broad-faced girl from Winnetka, Illinois, spent the summer teaching four- and five-year-olds in Ruleville. She said she ate her way out of her clothes. It was nerves, and the fear that each meal might be her last. Linda believes her Freedom School accomplished its work: "I think we taught some people, I really do. We would have done better if we had known more about rural Mississippi Negro children, but now we do, and this winter [the work in Mississippi goes on] we can put the experience to use."

In a backhanded way R. Gordon Burt Jr., the mayor of McComb, admitted their accomplishments: "Their school was a fizzle . . . F-I-Z-Z-L-E . . . nobody came but kids."

Thinking back on her summer, Linda said, "We've been living together, both races in the Negro community, and that's an accomplishment."

She's right. Mores and taboos could be seen being smashed all over the state as Mississippi whites learned that neither close association with Negroes nor bad food nor worse plumbing, any more than bombs, beatings, or arrests, could get the kids out. The place will never be the same.

The collegians didn't make it easier on themselves. They made no concessions to Mississippi sentiment on any subject.

The kids who were radical were no more bashful about it than the kids who were religious. They talked their radicalism "bodaciously," to use a Mississippi adverb, and you could find their copies of the leftish *National Guardian* on tabletops in civil rights headquarters all over the state.

Sometimes their dress was outlandish by Mississippi standards, sometimes just filthy by any standards. One white Mississippian, moved by the sight of an especially offensive pair, remarked, "Looks to me like they just heard about the Emancipation Proclamation and came right on down . . ."

Most were clean and reasonably dressed for fanning communities, but the ones that weren't bad high visibility, giving the state its first lesson in living and letting live with people you don't like and can't understand.

Many whites were taught no lesson they could learn this summer.

The white fraternity kids from Ole Miss and other state colleges who loaded Jackson's best motels every weekend to drink and fornicate under the eyes of adult chaperones, whose duty was to see the press didn't get pictures of Mississippi white youth disporting itself, learned little. One of them, a boy from Clarksdale, told me as he fondled a girl and a highball, "I was there the night of the troops [when the United States Army enforced the court-ordered integration of Ole Miss]. I was a freshman. I threw bricks and I wanted to hurt somebody."

Hartman Turnbow and his friends around Tchula learned much this summer. Before the civil rights organization sent him of the Negro delegates to the Democratic National Convention, where he and the others appeared like the ghost victims of an old crime, they had been going over to Lexington, the county seat, to "redish with the circus clerk," Holmes County version of "register with the circuit clerk."

Yet after he came back and told them about "the benefits of the meeting they carried on in Atlantic City, New Jersey," they had a new and personal appreciation of the American political process. The Negro people who live in Tchula and Mileston found his account of the politics interesting, but they also wanted to hear what it was like to be there, and he told them:

"I enjoyed the waves on the sandy beach and I liked to see them jumping toward me.

"We went to the California Hall, and I enjoyed that. There was seven ladies at a big table and they had seven big crocks of wine, and they laddled them out into little cups . . . as much as you want. Everybody was just smilin' and sippin' wine and talkin' to this one, that one, and the other one.

"We was walkin' and sippin' and I talked to the governor of California for fifteen minutes. There was lots of governors and senators.

"They were way out of my bracket, but the more wine they got under their belts, the more easy it was for us to make our arguments."

Farmer Turnbow told his neighbors about the politics of the convention as he understood them from "Bob Moes'" [Robert Moses], but the people seemed most absorbed in his account of his personal adventures with the great world, particularly with the reception given by Mrs. John F. Kennedy:

"We met the highest-class people in the United States and I didn't see any sign of one 'scriminating. As you go in you shakes hands with Mrs. Kennedy and you say anything you want.

"They put me down so low in Mississippi I thought I dreaming being with people with so much money and so much honor stored upon them. That Mrs. Kennedy had a reception for a bunch of Negroes that come back here and can't hardly eat. . . .

"I don't know what they gave me to drink but it was terrible good. I licked up a second glass but I didn't take a third 'cause I didn't want to show the Mississippi part of me. . . ."

The summer gave many Negroes hope, but it did not remove fear. They are especially afraid of reprisals once the Northerners go.

One night, walking down a country road, I was mistaken by a Negro for a civil rights worker. Coming up in the dark, he whispered a question many Negroes may be whispering:

"You're not going? You're not going away? You're going to stay with us, aren't you?"

Stay or go, the summer has not solved the problem of how the peace will be kept.

In many places the policemen are more dangerous than the civilians, and though one of the summer's fruits is the bringing of more FBI men than ever before, there still aren't enough, and often there is nothing they can do. Murder and mayhem are not in the federal jurisdiction.

In Mississippi you can be arrested for assault with intent to kill yourself when somebody tries to shoot you and you are a Negro. And, you must always be on your guard against the local government. Listen to the mayor of McComb sketch his plans for taking care of the civil rights workers:

"I'm not looking for the little things to give them harassment; I'm looking for the big arrest that will really give them trouble."

Nonetheless, one of the summer's accomplishments is forcing the police in the state into better behavior than they have displayed in the past. But how much does that mean when, during the summer, the FBI gave local authorities evidence proving one of their own policemen had shot a civil rights worker, and the man is still on the police force?

A great variety of people came to Mississippi during the summer of 1964. A goodly number were like the doctors who came because they felt they had to but, once there, didn't quite know what to do. The law prohibited them from practicing, although I did see a couple of them passing out aspirin and vitamin pills on the sly. They went about the state talking to local doctors and seeing all there was to see.

They would then congregate in a little second-floor Jackson's Farish Street, and there would tell each other about the filth of the charity hospital in Laurel, or that they had learned Negroes in Issaquena County are almost without medical care. They had the timidity of their profession, and scarcely ever said what they thought for publication, but presumably what they found will contribute to Northern integrationist fervor.

Some people found the summer profitless. The Leake County farmer's wife who said, "We're the last of our kind, the only members of our family left in farming," did not learn anything, because the past is already acted out and cannot be added to.

Some of those strong in will to do good did not learn. They are like Abe Osheroff, the Los Angeles carpenter with the face like a middle-aged bull with a new lease on life.

He put his family in hock, raised $10,000 from his friends, and came to Mississippi to build a community center, which he did, a fine one, professionally constructed, much better than the Negroes built for themselves over in Leake County. His was a gift to the people, but he did not learn to work with them.

This summer, many people who knew nothing of Mississippi before came and learned.

It was a summer in which the young redeemed the pledges of the old, in which the few justified the beliefs of the many.

ABOUT THE AUTHORS

Nicholas von Hoffman (1929–2018) was an American journalist and author. He worked as a community organizer for Saul Alinsky in Chicago and wrote for *The Washington Post*, among other publications.

Charles W. McKinney Jr. is associate professor of history at Rhodes College. He is author of *Greater Freedom: The Evolution of the Civil Rights Struggle in Wilson, North Carolina* and coeditor of *An Unseen Light: Black Struggles for Freedom in Memphis, Tennessee*, and *From Rights to Lives: The Evolution of the Black Freedom Struggle*.

ABOUT THE PHOTOGRAPHER

Henry Herr Gill (1930–2025) was a photojournalist who worked for the *Chicago Daily News* and the *Chicago Sun-Times*, among other newspapers. His work led to assignments in ninety-two countries, and his photographs and films in the world's hot spots have been highly acclaimed.